I NEVER FOUND THAT ROCKING CHAIR

God's Call at Retirement

RICHARD L. MORGAN

UPPER ROOM BOOKS
Nashville

I NEVER FOUND THAT ROCKING CHAIR
©1992 Richard L. Morgan.
All rights reserved.

Scripture quotations designated NIV are from *The Holy Bible, New International Version.* Copyright © 1973, 1978, 1984, International Bible Society and are used by permission of Zondervan Bible Publishers.

Scripture quotations designated JB are taken from *The Jerusalem Bible,* published and copyright © 1966, 1967, and 1968 by Darton, Longman & Todd Ltd. and Doubleday & Co. Inc., and are used by permission.

Scripture quotations designated NJB are taken from *The New Jerusalem Bible,* published and copyright © 1985 by Darton, Longman & Todd, Ltd. and Doubleday, a division of Bantam, Doubleday, Dell Publishing Group, Inc., and are used by permission.

Scripture quotations designated NKJV are from *The New King James Version.* copyright © 1979, 1980, 1982, Thomas Nelson Inc., Publishers and are used by permission.

Quotations marked RSV are from *The Revised Standard Version,* copyright © 1946, 1952, 1971 by the Division of Christian Education of the National Council of Churches of Christ in the USA and are used by permission.

Cover design: Bruce Gore for GORE STUDIOS (Nashville)
ISBN 0-8358-0663-4
Library of Congress Catalog Card Number: 92-61442
First printing: January, 1993 (10)
Printed in the USA.

DEDICATION

To those places
where retired people find redirection:

Quiet Libraries
Silent Woods and Lakes
The Presence of Soul-friends
The Holy Mystery

CONTENTS

Foreword

A FRIEND IN HIS SIXTIES recently shared with me his distress about retirement. He is looking forward to leaving his job in the public school system but is frightened by the pattern he sees among his retired friends. Their days, he says, seem filled with endless golf games and a kind of purposelessness. My friend confesses to liking golf but finds it hard to imagine spending his days that way for very long. His questions about the use of his time open out into deeper concerns: Will I have a reason to get up in the morning if I don't have to report to my job? Is everything slipping away from me–my physical well-being, my friends, my energy? How do I find a sense of direction? Where is God in all of this? This book is a gentle and wise guide for my friend and all who ponder their retirement years.

As women and men prepare for retirement, they can usually find resources for financial planning and leisure activities. But these are often not the most troublesome aspects of retirement. The critical search is for the significance of these years, their place in the spiritual journey we began in childhood. That is why I am happy to welcome books like Richard Morgan's to the literature on aging. Morgan takes us further than the usual discussions of money, educational and travel opportunities, good nutrition, volunteering, and second careers. He shows us how retirement (*redirection*, as he prefers) is a spiritual passage. He helps us find God in it. He shows us how to make sense of the retirement experience and live it with courage and meaning.

Aging is an ambiguous experience. As we grow older we can discover a new freedom and simplicity and find the grace of the present moment. We can learn to enjoy solitude, expand our compassion, and enter more deeply into ourselves and life. But the last decades of life challenge and puzzle us too. We experience losses that threaten to break us: our spouse of many years, close and irreplaceable friends, physical health, and the identity that came from our work. These losses call us to examine again all the values that have sustained our lives. Might my worth depend finally on who I am rather than on what I do? Can I find God in times of weakness and failure as well as in times of strength and success? How we answer these questions is crucial not only for ourselves but for all the generations whose lives are intertwined. Our children and grandchildren need such answers as much as we do.

I Never Found That Rocking Chair offers insights into all of these aspects of spirituality. Morgan, a long-time student of the literature on spirituality and aging, weaves his learning quietly into his reflections. His background in the field and long pastoral experience ground his meditations in the best of contemporary thinking on this topic. He shows us how it feels from within, day after day, to faithfully live out the passage of retirement. His experiences are set in the context of the biblical story, from which, in an original way, he draws insight with special relevance to later years.

As he finds his way into the lived conviction that retirement is a time of vital involvement and creative prayer, Richard Morgan is glad–and so are we–that he never found that rocking chair. Instead, he found a way to offer his experience to others, and so make the passage of retirement easier and richer for them. The combination of biblical passages, personal reflection, and prayer make it ideal for using the book as a way to start each day. Or give it to friends you care about. And as a gift, it is a surer guide to the meaning of retirement than the traditional gold watch has ever been.

Kathleen Fischer

Preface

YOU MAY BE READING THIS BOOK because you are retired, and yet feel a sense of uneasiness and emptiness about your life. I know how you feel. There were times in my retirement when I wished I had never left my work. You may be reading this book because you will face retirement soon and you are experiencing some anxiety about this major life change. I know that feeling too. I remember even now the distress, almost panic I felt when I made that awesome decision.

You may be reading this book because you are an adult child of an older parent who is retired, or will retire soon. You need to understand their feelings. You may be reading this book because even in a happy retirement there is always the haunting question, What does God have to do with these years? It was only later that I realized how God had called me to this new journey of life's Third Age. Whoever you are, if retirement has touched your life, this book is for you.

Taken from journals I kept during the retirement process, my story seeks to help those who seek a spiritual understanding of this transition. For retirement *is* a paradox, near and yet so distant, probable and yet so impossible to imagine. Paul Tournier says, "People are so absorbed in their work, sometimes so deadened by it, that retirement takes them by surprise."

Hopefully, reading this story of retirement will prepare you for your journey, and convince you that retirement needs to be redefined as an opportunity for new directions in a future God has planned for you.

Richard L. Morgan

I

MAKING THE
AWESOME DECISION

*People are
so absorbed in their work,
sometimes so deadened by it,
that retirement takes them by surprise.
They have not furnished their lives
with durable goods which will still be there when
their work has gone.
That is what preparation for retirement is.
It means living in a way
which prepares for an old age
which will be a broadening of life.*

PAUL TOURNIER

When Is The Right Time?

READ ECCLESIASTES 3:1-8

There is a time for everything,
and a season for every activity under heaven.
(Ecclesiastes 3:1, NIV)

THE GREEKS HAD TWO WORDS FOR DESIGNATING TIME. One was *chronos*, clock time, the time measured by hours and days. The other was *kairos*, unique moments in time when something significant happens. Most of us judge our lives in terms of *chronos*, the moments defined by clocks and calendars. We seldom take time to find time. But, each of us can remember *kairos*, the holy moments when something special happened to us.

So, I ask myself, "When is the *right time* to retire?" The *chronos* is right, because I am aware of my need to withdraw from the world of work into a slowed down, redirected life. But is it God's *kairos* for me?

Two gifts are required if I am to understand if this is the right time for me to retire. The first is the gift of discernment. I must be alert to God's nudges, to that inner voice that beckons me to this new direction in life's journey.

The prophet Elijah found God not in "the earthquake, wind, and fire, but in the still, small voice." That openness to God's call must have shown Elijah that it was time to turn over the mantle to Elisha. (See 2 Kings 2.)

The second gift is that of patience. It is too easy to force the right time, to blunder ahead into new directions without divine guidance. Patience requires that I wait until the time is right, and often that means silent anticipation and ceaseless prayer.

Now I know. It is the *kairos* for my retirement. I have taken care of the *chronos* events–finances, place to live, new hobbies. But, now I know that it is God's time for me to begin this journey of the Third Age of life. We can make all the right decisions about finances, where to live, part-time work; but there is still much inner emotional work needed. Unknown pitfalls and opportunities await. I know I am saying my good-byes to a meaningful active professional life, and I have no idea of what it will be like to be "retired."

But, I know God has gone before me into this new stage of life, and the word that came to that ancient people, who faced an unknown future, becomes a *kairos* word.

Have I not commanded you? Be strong, and of good courage; be not frightened, neither be dismayed; for the LORD your God is with you wherever you go.
–Joshua 1:9, RSV

It is the right time.

GRACIOUS GOD:
You are our sure support and strength
in all of life's varied experiences. Our comfort comes in
knowing that whatever faces us in this life,
we can be sure of your presence.
AMEN.

Proactive Retirement
READ LUKE 16:1-9

The master praised the dishonest steward
for looking ahead; for the children of this world
look further ahead, in dealing with their own generation
than the children of light.
(Luke 16:9, MOFFATT)

THERE ARE FEW PARABLES OF JESUS which are more puzzling than the story of the dishonest steward. It seems inconsistent with Jesus' values, as it commends dishonesty and shady ethics. Knowing that he was about to be fired, this shrewd manager devised a scheme to cover his deceit and protect his future when he was out of work.

By reducing the bills of some of his master's debtors, he incurred their gratitude, and assured himself of a place to go when he was fired. He was praised for the wisdom of his foresight. He adjusted his behavior to meet the future. He looked ahead.

Jesus always admired and praised foresight, ingenuity and resourcefulness. He praised the five wise maidens who remembered to buy oil in advance of the wedding feast, and the man who had the foresight to sell all that he had and buy a field because treasure was hidden in it.

This parable makes us realize that if a grafter, faced with a uncertain future, can think clearly, plan ahead, and act resourcefully in his own interest, how much more should Christians act with prudence regarding their future security. The writer of the Proverbs said it well, "those who plan good have joy." (See Proverbs 12:20.)

Planning for retirement is a Christian act. We are called to make our retirement years "the best third of our life." But it takes planning. So I have participated in several retirement planning seminars, and have carefully planned for financial security, insurance and health protection, and other legal matters. But I am still haunted by the fear of the unknown.

I have been through an endless array of check-lists and self-administered quizzes about retirement, and tried to be as prudent as that manager in the parable about protecting my future. But still a fear persists. What about all that free time? What will it feel like to no longer be defined by what I do? How will I cope without a full-time job?

Reacting to the multitude of retirement planning seminars, Jules Z. Willing says, "All this is so sensible, practical and thorough that he is misled into thinking that he understands retirement and is prepared for it. All these activities do constitute the *business* of *arranging* retirement, but almost none of it touches on the *experience of becoming* a retired person."

I have planned ahead for my retirement, but there is a part of me that wonders what it will be like. And even more important, how will it all fit into my calling as a Christian? What could God want me to do with this gift of freedom?

PROTECTOR OF ALL WHO TRUST:
Help us to be as wise in preparing for our future,
as was the manager in Jesus' parable. Even more, help us to
put our ultimate trust in you, the God who is our keeper,
the God who neither slumbers, nor sleeps.
AMEN.

3

Anxious Moments
READ MATTHEW 6:24-34

"Who of you by worrying can add a single hour to his life?
Therefore do not worry about tomorrow,
for tomorrow will worry about itself.
Each day has enough trouble of its own."
(Matthew 6:27, 34, NIV)

YESTERDAY I READ A POEM about retirement in Peggy Shriver's book, *Pinches of Salt.*

> His step had slowed,
> feet plodding through a silt of year.
> His mind, aware of now,
> double-exposed it with the past.
> Committees met, shook heads, and hands,
> and gave him to the past–
> The dead past.
> And so he died.

The poem evoked all kinds of feelings within me, as I plan for my retirement in a few weeks. I certainly experienced some genuine anxiety.

Of course for some time I had suffered from depletion and anxiety, that profound uneasiness that overtakes a person when he or she feels that life is slipping away. One of the reasons I chose to retire was to beat burnout, and get out of the pressure while there was still time.

But now a gnawing sense of anxiety gripped me. Had I made the right decision? If anxiety is a threat to some value that a person holds essential to their existence as a person, I had a right to be anxious. Since the day I was fifteen, I had been immersed in the world of work. What I did–the projects I completed, the work I accomplished–had defined my existence. Now, in a retirement ceremony to be held soon (it will probably seem more like a funeral), I will receive the golden handshakes from my colleagues, and it will be over. My past will be gone. What about the present? Will I eke out my days watching old reruns or waiting for the evening paper? I never did play golf and I don't expect to begin now.

These are anxious moments. Of all the fears, none is worse than fear of the unknown. If only I knew what to expect. But it all seems gray and distant. I know Paul said, "Never be anxious" (Philippians 4:6, MOFFATT), but I am prone to anxiety, if not paralyzed by it.

But, I resolve to take a step at a time, to not worry about tomorrow, to believe the gospel, and to trust God. With Teresa of Avila I pray:

> Let nothing disturb thee;
> Nothing affright thee;
> All things are passing;
> God never changeth;
> Patient endurance
> Attaineth to all things;
> Who God possesseth
> In nothing is wanting;
> Alone God sufficeth.

ROCK OF OUR LIFE:
We are so unstable,
carried to and fro by every contrary wind that comes our way.
Help us to find deep peace in your presence
and healing in your love.
AMEN.

4

Jesus Never Planned His Retirement

READ PSALM 90

Our days dwindle under your wrath,
our lives are over in a breath. . . .
Teach us to count how few days we have
and so gain wisdom of heart.
(Psalm 90:9,12, JB)

IN ONE OF THOSE MARATHON SESSIONS at a retirement planning seminar, I felt overwhelmed by all the endless data about financial planning, medical insurance, and pension plans. A jarring thought flooded my mind–Jesus never planned his retirement! His thoughts about last things focused more on his death and resurrection.

Jesus gave no thought to deferred annuities or investments. His only property was a seamless robe. His estate consisted of a vacant cross and a borrowed empty tomb. This carpenter of Nazareth would not look forward to sunny retirement days with friends and family, protected by social security and guaranteed years of relaxed living.

Yet, I believe that Jesus would affirm our planning for retirement. After all, he cautioned the maidens in the parable to be prepared with oil for the coming of the bridegroom. But his simple life and quiet poverty make me feel uncomfortable with all the clatter about material things. I remembered another parable about a rich farmer who was so prosperous that he decided to retire in style, and enjoy life. "You have plenty of good things laid up for many years. Take life easy; eat, drink, and be merry," he said to himself (Luke 12:19, NIV). Like the crack of lightning in a summer night, all those grandiose plans for travel and relaxation went up in smoke. God said, "This very night your life will be demanded from you. Then who will get what you have prepared for yourself?" (Luke 12:20, NIV).

The ancient psalmist counseled us to do more than simply pay attention to the time we may have left to live or to be sure we are materially secure. "Gain a wisdom of heart" means to make each day count and live it from the depths. This "heart of wisdom" is rarely possible during our earlier frantic years. Our days and nights then are crowded with deadlines to meet, achievements to pursue, bills to pay and property to maintain.

Retirement offers us a final chance to reverse this life of rush and acquisition. We do need to prepare wisely for retirement, but we must not neglect the spiritual realities. "Man does not live on bread alone, but on every word that comes from the mouth of God" (Matthew 4:4, NIV). Even in the throes of all this retirement planning, the presence of the One who "though he was rich, yet for your sakes he became poor, so that you through his poverty might become rich" (2 Corinthians 8:9, NIV) became real to me. And I vowed not to be rich in things and poor in soul. I would be spiritually prepared too!

MOST MERCIFUL GOD:
You love us with an everlasting love,
even when we forget where life's treasures really exist.
Help us to wisely lay up treasures in heaven,
and to find our real joy in you.
AMEN.

Time to Leave, Not Cleave
READ RUTH 1:1-21

Then Naomi said to her two daughters-in-law, "Go back, each of you, to your mother's home. May the LORD show kindness to you . . . . Then Orpah kissed her mother-in-law good-by. (Ruth 1:8, 14, NIV)

I KNEW IT WAS TIME to leave. I was nearing burnout and the burden was becoming unbearable. Quit while you are ahead, the saying goes. It was, as Joyce Rupp would say, time to pray my good-byes. I was at that place in life when we find ourselves without a something or someone that has given our life meaning and value.

I had mixed emotions, to say the least. There was sadness that it would soon be over. Part of me was still unfulfilled, as though there was something yet to happen in my world of work. My good-bye would not only be to friends and routines, but to a way of life.

But, there was some joy that I could escape the stress. No longer would I hear the same old issues rephrased, rehashed, and replayed. No more need to placate persons in power, to play endless survival games, and to keep looking nervously over my shoulder to see if someone was gaining on me. I would now taste freedom–from appointments that end in disappointment and meetings where people never met.

I felt empathy for Orpah, the daughter-in-law who said good-bye to Naomi. Oddly, her story has been untold. We have idealized Ruth's decision to stay with Naomi and follow the call of a new God. But, we have ignored the courage of Orpah who chooses another path. Caught between the cultures, she has her story to tell and we need to affirm her decision to leave rather than cling to Naomi.

In her book *Praying Our Goodbyes*, Joyce Rupp writes:

> What is a good-bye? It is an empty place in us. It is any situation in which there is some kind of loss, some incompleteness, when a space is created in us that cries out to be filled. . . . Good-byes are all of those experiences that leave us with a hollow feeling someplace deep inside.

I am now saying good-bye to thirty-seven years of ministry, and there is a hollow feeling.

I have participated in retirement planning seminars, done all the proper planning that the experts advise. But I still feel some terror at the unknown which awaits. Part of me still wants to cling to my old identity, for this is what defined my existence. Like Orpah, I know the time has come to cut those lifelong work strings and forge ahead in new directions.

Though I tremble on the edge of a "maybe" (this new thing called retirement), I have no plans and no panic. I have no idea of what I will *do* in the next few months, but I know who I will *be*. The time has come to leave. With the writer of the hymn "Lead Kindly Light" I sing:

> I do not ask to see the distant scene–
> One step enough for me.

AWESOME GOD:
I feel terror at leaving the work which has been so much of who I am. The future seems like a blur. I have no idea of what lies ahead. I know only that you are there.
AMEN.

6

Fearing the Unknown
READ JOSHUA 1:1-9

Have I not commanded you?
Be strong and of good courage; do not be afraid,
nor be dismayed, for the LORD your God is
with you wherever you go.
(Joshua 1:9, NKJV)

NO FEAR HAUNTS MORE than the fear of the unknown. Whether it be facing a new job or relocating our home or the dread we feel before surgery or awaiting results of medical tests, it stalks our path all our days.

The Israelites stood ready to cross the river and claim their destiny. Behind them were memories of sacrifices and lessons learned in the wilderness. Before them was the fear of the unknown. They only needed to recall the spies' report of giants in the land, before whom they would be as grasshoppers. Some Israelites may have had misgivings about Joshua's leadership and mourned the loss of Moses, wondering how they could go on without him. Change brings fear of the unknown.

Retirement creates endless fears of the unknown. Moving into it has been as staggering as going from dependence on parents to self-supporting adulthood or from life with a spouse alone to the responsibilities of children. After the excitement of the early days has ended, questions begin to come: What will it be like to no longer be employed and deprived of the challenges that work brings? Will there be any threatening illnesses that may come? Or financial problems? What will it be like to plan my own week, after so much of my time being programmed by others? It looks like retirement will take more initiative than working. Do I face endless days and nights of depression and uncertainty? It *will* be different.

The life of the Christian is always uncertain. There are no guarantees. Paul tells the Ephesian elders at a time of change in his life, "And now, compelled by the Spirit, I am going to Jerusalem, not knowing what will happen to me there" (Acts 20:22, NIV). *Going* and *Not Knowing* seems to be the paradigm of the life of faith. But in the unknown places, God is there before you.

God reassured Joshua and his people that they would not be alone in that unknown land. God is not only the God who comes to our help when we have plunged into the unknown. On the dimmest and farthest trails, God is the One who is always there first.

In *The Denial of Death,* Ernest Becker argues that the fear of death, the cosmic unknown, is present beneath all the appearances of living. How appropriate that on the first Easter, when the women came to the tomb, sorrowful that their future is bleak and worried about who would roll away the stone from the tomb, God had been there first. The words of "Peace, Perfect Peace in this Dark World of Sin" are true:

> Peace, perfect peace, our future all unknown?
> Jesus we know, and He is on the throne.

BLESSED GOD:
*We are like children who fear
the darkness at night, afraid of unknown terrors.
As we move through this new unknown in our lives, grant us
the awareness of your sure presence and protection.*
AMEN.

Let Me Be Me
READ 1 SAMUEL 17:31-40

By the grace of God, I am what I am . . . .
(1 Corinthians 15:10, RSV)

I HAD TO GET NEW BUSINESS CARDS PRINTED, and it dawned on me that for over thirty-five years I was defined by what I did. Former business cards had stated that I was a minister or counselor or chaplain. Now, who am I? I shied away from putting "retired" on the card and was tempted to put "aging specialist." I ended up just with my name and address.

One of the reasons I refused to use the term "retired" on that card is that many people still confuse retirement with aging. I prefer the term *Third Age* since it connotes a person who is active, in reasonably good health, with time and energy for vital involvement. To me, it is *Old Age* that is the time at the end of life, when one is plagued with the inevitable frailties of old age.

It feels good to be who I am. At age seventy, May Sarton said "I am more myself than I have ever been." It is so easy to allow yourself to be programmed by others' expectations and demands. I have always appreciated the fact that David refused to wear the armor of Saul in his epic struggle against Goliath. Although the helmet of brass and coat of mail seemed good protection, he preferred his own weapons, the shepherd skills he learned in the wilderness, and his reliance on Yahweh. David had to be himself, not a mirror of the King. Life seems to be a struggle for this same sense of identity, especially when society and others want to make us into their image.

Years ago, in the disruption of a painful divorce, I had to rediscover who I was. Even a bad marriage identifies your existence. I was brought back full circle to where I started, and only after months of hard work gained a new sense of my real self. Now, once again, I find myself in an identity crisis, separated from my roles in the world of work.

Strange as it may seem, it feels good to simply be me, to be a human being, not a human doing. Centuries ago, Job said "Naked I came from my mother's womb, and naked I will depart" (Job 1:21, NIV). All we take into the next world is the person we have become. The Third Age is a time of stripping away all masks and illusions and facing ourselves honestly without pretense.

"By the grace of God I am what I am," wrote Paul. And I am confident that the loss of my work identity will mean greater growth and maturity. One sure thing, I now celebrate a deeper truth: No one ever "earns" his or her way, who we are is more a gift of God's grace than a function of our achievement.

GRACIOUS GOD:
I am content in being a person,
a person redeemed and transformed by your grace.
Let me realize the unsearchable riches in Christ Jesus,
and the marvelous gift of love.
AMEN.

8

At The Social Security Office
READ PSALM 139 & PSALM 121

Strengthen the feeble hands,
steady the knees that give way; say to those with fearful
hearts; "Be strong, do not fear; your God will come."
(Isaiah 35:3-4, NIV)

IT IS FIVE DAYS BEFORE CHRISTMAS, the birth of "peace on earth." But I feel so anxious as I sit in the Social Security Office and wait for the final interview. It all seems so final. There is no turning back now. This was my decision and I made a free choice. All my plans have been made, but it still is scary to think about the curtain coming down on my career.

My career began forty-five years ago in a paint brush factory and now it ends in a government office. I think endlessly about all the years of work and how I measured my life by achievements and successes. The ancient prophet knew what it meant to be anxious, to have feeble hands, shaking knees, and a fearful heart. But his counsel was, "God will come."

I thought how ironic it is that retirees are given watches when they retire. We need no clock to remind us that time is one thing we will have on our hands. We will have more than enough time to wander where we like, time to walk alone in quiet streets, and time to reflect on what life has meant.

I can't escape the feeling that my decision to retire was not just my own doing. It is as if Another pointed me in this direction. But where is God now, as I wait in this Advent season, in this gathering darkness, as I wait for the Word to be made flesh?

In ancient Israel, some of the neighboring tribes believed that the gods were restricted to certain localities; their presence could only be known in holy places or on certain hills or mountains. But the God of Israel was not so limited. As Stephen told his accusers, "The Most High does not live in houses made by men" (Acts 7:48, NIV). God's presence is everywhere, as much at a social security office as in the sanctuary, as real at retirement as at ordination. The words of Psalm 139 (NIV) resounded in my heart,

> Where can I go from your Spirit?
> Where can I flee from your presence?
> If I go up to the heavens, you are there;
> If I make my bed in the depths, you are there.
> If I rise on the wings of the dawn,
> if I settle on the far side of the sea,
> even there your hand will guide me,
> your right hand will hold me fast.

In the depths. On the far side of the sea. It certainly seems that way at this moment. But one must take courage in God's presence even here, even at this moment when the decision is being set in stone.

ETERNAL KEEPER:
Retirement is a moment of transition on Life's journey.
We take courage in the knowledge that you are our Keeper
and will watch over our coming and going
both now and forevermore.
AMEN.

II

EXPERIENCING THE FIRST FREEDOM

The feeling of retirement,
at first, is like the feeling of playing hooky.
Naughty. Nice. . . .

Then comes the day we discover the truth
that Mark Twain's Huckleberry Finn
discovered before us:
hooky-playing as a way of life is
boring.

HOWARD SHANK

The Joy of Doing Nothing
READ MARK 4:30-34

What shall we say the kingdom of God is like?
It is like a mustard seed, which is the smallest seed you plant
in the ground. Yet when planted, it grows and
becomes the largest of all garden plants.
(Mark 4:30-32, NIV)

ONE OF THE EARLY JOYS OF RETIREMENT is the freedom to do nothing. I have revised the old advice to say, "Don't do anything; just stand there." No clocks concern me; no crowded calendars stifle my creativity. My keys feel lighter; I even put a letter to my former parish in the "out of town" box.

It seems strange for a lifelong workaholic. I have always set clear boundaries, thrived on deadlines, and lived my life between schedules. Now I begin to realize the meaning of the saying, "He does not seem to me to be a free man, who does not sometimes do nothing."

I know our culture places a premium on busyness. I have been programmed to believe that idleness is a great sin. Some of my colleagues even warned me that, "Nothing can be as dangerous as retiring. Doing nothing can kill you."

But I am enjoying the respite. Most of the time, I don't have to be somewhere at a proper time. I don't have to prod myself to accommodate others' agendas. I can just do nothing.

So often I have lived my life like an overpacked suitcase, bursting at the seams. Bound by the grave clothes of routine, it has been a stylized life. As I reflect on it all now, so much of it seems nothing more than spinning wheels. Yet, as I do nothing, the miracle is that God is at work in my stillness. I remember the parable of the mustard seed. It lies secretly in the ground, seemingly so insignificant. But in time the tiny seed sprouts and becomes a glorious bush. Jesus reminds us that our worth does not depend on the world's values but on God's work.

In these days, I begin to realize again what the gospel means. I may be doing nothing, but God is at work in my life. I am reminded of the ancient prophet Habakkuk who had to wait for his answer.

> For still the vision awaits its time;
> it hastens to the end–it will not lie.
> If it seems slow, wait for it;
> it will surely come; it will not delay.

I don't know yet what the vision for my future may be–but I am learning patience, and the joy of doing nothing.

I take seriously the counsel of Psalm 46. In the midst of a time of panic, when the "waters roar and are troubled, and the mountains quake with their surging," the psalmist urged, "Be still, and know that I am God." I am learning the joy of doing nothing.

GOD OUR HELPER:
You are so active in our lives and yet we fail to recognize your work because we are so preoccupied with our concerns. Thank you for helping us realize that it's good to do nothing. Help us to commit our days into your hands.
AMEN.

Getting Unstressed
READ JOHN 16:25-33

*I have said this to you, that in me you may have peace.
In the world you have tribulation; but be of good cheer,
I have overcome the world.*
(John 16:33 RSV)

TODAY, FOR THE FIRST TIME IN SOME TIME, I left my watch on the dresser and went a full day without being controlled by that clock. Clock time has often dictated my day, beset with deadlines, meeting times, and scheduled appointments. What a relief to be free from that master.

My stress level has been greatly reduced. No doubt I may miss some of the *eustress* (good stress) that creates energy and provides satisfaction. But I will never miss the *distress* (bad stress) that causes all manner of wear and tear on our lives. We are just beginning to realize how much distress is a major factor in all of the major diseases.

A recent study showed that workplace stress causes thirty-four per cent of workers to consider quitting their jobs. In the same study, jobs are cited by twenty-seven per cent of the participants as the single greatest stress factor, ahead of divorce and other traumas. The last years at work created mega-stress for me. All too present were danger signs: overwork, conflicting demands, emotional strain, physical symptoms. Now that this major stressor in my life is gone, I feel so much more at ease, free from dis-ease.

As Christians living in an alien world, we will always have distress. Jesus warned us that "In the world you will have trouble," *but*, "be of good cheer, I have overcome the world." Occupations can become preoccupations, and the resulting distress can make us so distracted that we lose sight of our faith.

These early days of the redirected life are helping me to center myself, to be attentive, and to be present to those spiritual realities that one manages somehow to miss in daily activities. At last there is time for solitude and quiet walks in lonely places, and I am learning the wisdom of Jesus' words: "Come away by yourselves to a lonely place, and rest a while" (Mark 6:31, RSV).

Other stressors will appear in time. But for the moment I am getting unstressed. It is painful to realize that most of our stress is caused by our own lack of trust. But, retirement gives you the opportunity to make a new beginning with simple trust in the One who has overcome the world.

The words of contemporary writer David Mowbray mean much to me now.

> Lord of our older years,
> Steep thought the road may be,
> Rid us of foolish fears,
> Bring us serenity;
> Your grace surrounds us all our days;
> For all your gifts we bring our praise..

SOURCE OF PEACE:
Teach us to rely on your grace for freedom from distress.
We are born for trouble as the sparks fly upward, but nothing
is so powerful that it detracts from your adequacy.
AMEN.

Tasting Freedom
READ GALATIANS 5:1-13

When Yahweh brought Zion's captives home,
at first it seemed like a dream;
then our mouths filled with laughter and our lips with song.
(Psalm 126:1-2, JB)

HOWARD SHANK SPEAKS THE TRUTH when he claims that the first feelings of retirement are like playing hooky from school. "It delights our spirit to do anything the working class can't. To ignore the alarm clock, duck the rush hour, let the telephone ring, stop the paper avalanche. To play, to loaf." It is a great feeling to experience this new freedom.

The ancient Israelites had feelings of exaltation and joy at their new freedom to worship at Jerusalem. Their return from exile was like a dream, too good to be true. No longer controlled by their captors and their taunts, now they were free to praise their Lord.

The early Christians in the Galatian churches also celebrated their freedom from the demands of the Law and their gracious acceptance by God. The gospel had liberated them from the tyranny of making themselves accepted to God and freed them to live by grace. This freedom gave them energy to reshape the world.

For days now, I have wanted to pinch myself to make sure I am not in some dream world. This freedom is incredible. My lifestyle for so long had been largely a matter of conformity–following the expectations and demands of others. Now I am free to be myself, to know I am accepted for who I am, to explore my own options, and to set my own priorities.

On the day he retired, Horace Whittell of Gillingham, England, brought to work the alarm clock that had roused him at six o'clock for forty-seven years. He placed the clock on the concrete, climbed into an eighty-ton press, and drove over the noisemaker. He said, "It was a lovely feeling."

Even now I know that this is the "honeymoon stage" of retirement and that this euphoric feeling won't last. But for now, I will bask in this feeling. Throughout the journey of life we seek to be free, but the strange paradox is that the more we are successful, the less we are free. Freedom seems to be an elusive will-o-wisp that slips through our fingers. I am also grateful for my financial security and always bear in mind that for some who retire, mere survival replaces the luxury of freedom I enjoy.

I know now that there is a vast difference between retirement and aging. Being retired, experiencing this new freedom, feeling some control over my choices, makes me feel younger. Satchel Paige, the ageless baseball pitcher used to say, "How old would you be if you didn't know how old you was?" Many "old" people are still at work, and many retired persons do not feel old.

For now, I am like those Hebrews who rejoiced in the moment of freedom newly found. It is time to laugh, to celebrate, to dance.

SOURCE OF ALL TRUE JOY:
We pause to thank you for your gifts of the Spirit.
For this sense of freedom, for this deliverance,
we give you our heartfelt thanks.
AMEN.

Redeemed from John Henryism
READ HEBREWS 4:1-13

For anyone who enters God's rest
also rests from his own work, just as God did from his.
Let us, therefore, make every effort to enter that rest.
(Hebrews 4:10-11, NIV)

MOST REMEMBER THE STORY OF JOHN HENRY, the best steel-driving man on the railroad. When a machine came along to do his job, he swore he could outperform steam power any day. In a contest, John Henry did indeed beat the machine and then collapsed with a ruptured blood vessel in his head. Not exactly a successful end to his career.

Social scientists call the kind of hard work that always promises success, no matter what: *John Henryism.* John Henry is determined to climb to the top, regardless of the cost to himself or his family. He adds project after project to an already full plate. He strives incessantly, a type-A personality who wants control. His stress level is very high. Some medical professionals estimate that sixty percent of doctors' visits are stress-related. Wearing down the body weakens the immune system and can hasten the progress of life-threatening illness such as heart disease and cancer.

I suffered from John Henryism in the parish. I liked tackling things other people couldn't do and at times I was overbearing, if not abrasive. I salved my conscience with pious thoughts that it was God's work and must be done. The reality is that the more we succeed, the more we strive. I am not minimizing the need for results. My frenetic striving achieved the building of three major buildings in ten years. But it is too easy to substitute results for growth and sacrifice spiritual reality for success. At the end of a project, I asked myself: "Am I willing to sacrifice power and projects for peace and the life of the soul?" I knew the answer. I could not stay in the parish and not be John Henry.

I have experienced an incredible freedom these days. I am experiencing what the writer to the Hebrews meant by God's rest. This rest is both a present reality and a future hope. God's people can enter the promised experience of rest now, but rest in its fullness is yet to be achieved. What is this rest? It is the joy of salvation in Jesus Christ, already a reality for Christians, but which will become an even deeper dimension in the eternal life of the people of God. "There remains, then, a Sabbath-rest for the people of God" (Hebrews 4:9, NIV).

Part of the new freedom I am experiencing is deliverance from the compulsive need to achieve at any cost. It becomes an endless cycle, leading to stress, disappointment and frustration. Some of my problem comes from past programming that my worth is measured by what I achieve rather than who I become. It's not that I don't have any goals, I do. The difference is that I am investing myself in things that I enjoy and that accentuate my strengths.

God has saved me from John Henryism. I am going to get out of the steam engine's way and be myself.

GREAT HEALER OF BODY AND SOUL:
We confess our refusals to rest
and our preoccupation with restless striving after success.
Grant us the peace and joy that comes
as we center ourselves in your love.
AMEN.

Learning Simplicity
READ PHILIPPIANS 4:10-13

*I have learned the secret of being content
in any and every situation, whether well fed or hungry,
whether living in plenty or in want.
I can do everything through him who gives me strength.
(Philippians 4:12-13, NIV)*

I AM AMAZED AT HOW OFTEN I have recently said to myself, "I am learning the difference between what I want and what I need." Living on a reduced income means that you have to simplify your life. I realize that much of the wisdom of the Christian life can be found in living simply.

Paul said, "I have learned the secret of being content in any and every situation" (Philippians 4:12, NIV). Paul learned that true contentment was found in himself, and not in things or events. He could be at peace, whatever the situation. He was not defeated by poverty or ruined by plenty. He did not collapse under the strain of stress, yet he did not get too high over success. He could be just as content as a prisoner in a Roman jail as he was in preaching the gospel in the open streets of Corinth.

Retirement paves the way for a simpler life style. Socrates once walked down the streets of Athens, looked into the shop windows, and marveled at what he could do without. I have found real joy in clearing out some clutter and in giving things away to friends or charities. It takes grace to practice the words of Jesus,

"Give to him who begs from you, and do not refuse him who would borrow from you" (Matthew 5:42, RSV). Richard has written, "Develop a habit of giving things away. If you find that you are becoming attached to some possession, consider giving it to someone who needs it."

Practicing this simple way of living has reopened my eyes to the beauties of nature. I have become closer to the earth, seen anew the beauty of God's world, marveled endlessly at the rich colors of a winter sky. Simplicity means that we rediscover that, "The heavens declare the glory of God; the skies proclaim the work of his hands. Day after day they pour forth speech; night after night they display knowledge" (Psalm 19:1-2, NIV).

Simplicity delivers us from the tyranny of things. What one *is* does not depend on what one *has*. As Jesus said, "a man's life does not consist in the abundance of his possessions" (Luke 12:15, RSV). Being willing to be known for who we are, we are not under the constraint of resorting to things to justify our importance. No wonder Thoreau said, "Simplify, simplify."

These first days of retirement have taught me that only the simple are the free. Everyone else is under the tyranny of our demands for recognition and for things. And simplicity is a gift from the One whose life was a paragon of simplicity. "I can do all things in him who strengthens me" (Philippians 4:13, RSV).

GIVER OF ALL GOOD THINGS:
We praise you for the constant
gifts of gentleness and love that grace our lives.
Now give us the will to simplify those lives.
AMEN.

14

Rest for The Weary
READ JOHN 4:1-42

---

*Come to Me, all you who labor and are heavy laden,
and I will give you rest.
Take My yoke upon you, and learn from Me,
for I am gentle and lowly in heart,
and you will find rest for your souls.
(Matthew 11:28-29, NKJV)*

THE WOMAN OF SAMARIA came to Jacob's well in the burning noontime heat, worn out from life. Her life was trapped in a non-fulfilling cycle of filling and emptying water jars, marrying and divorcing and remarrying. When this Stranger spoke to her of "living water" she said to him, "Sir, give me this water so that I won't get thirsty and have to keep coming here to draw water" (John 4:15, NIV). Her dried up life and the restlessness in her soul created a thirst for peace and rest.

I can identify with her feelings. Worn down by years of work and ministry, weary of the drudgery of it all, and at times allowing religious matters to stifle my soul, I needed living water. As Augustine prayed, "Our hearts are restless until they rest in Thee."

What transformed the woman's life was the acceptance and love of this Jesus. "Come, see a man who told me everything I ever did" (John 4:29, NIV). This Person understands me. She left her water jar at the well for she didn't need it anymore. She now had "living water."

I am experiencing a marvelous sense of peace and rest in this redirected life. Freed from the pressures of full time work, I make time now for prayer and reflection. In the ability to rest lies the secret of facing and mastering the most profound things of the soul. I can leave the old water jars at the well, and I can let the living water nourish my soul. I can be quiet now, and I can hear voices I could not always hear amid all the noise that came before.

Is it not symbolic that this living water was found at Jacob's well? It was only in a life of struggle that Jacob discovered God's peace. His conversion from Jacob to Israel came when God blessed him in the midnight struggle of the soul. No longer driven by ambition or consumed by his desires for power, he found serenity of soul.

Christ does give rest. Not a way of escape from the world, but a deep, inner peace in the midst of life. We need only heed that invitation to come to him, to lay down our yokes, and take his yoke upon us. It is available to anyone, at any time. For me, it took these slowed down days of early retirement to lay down the yoke of the staleness of life and find this living water.

OUR REFUGE AND STRENGTH:
Our only true rest is found in you.
Calm our restless spirits, cleanse us of distracted living,
and center us, once and for all, in your peace.
AMEN.

Keeping Life Out of Stopping Places

READ LUKE 9:28-35

As the men were leaving Jesus, Peter said to him,
"Master, it is good for us to be here.
Let us put up three shelters. . . .
(He did not know what he was saying.)
(Luke 9:33, NIV)

I REMEMBER AS A CHILD how I loved to ride the merry-go-round at the seashore park. You would think that five rides on the merry-go-round would be enough. But I kept begging my parents to ride again, until finally I said, "I want to live on a merry-go-round." There were times in my career when I think that wish came true! My parents wisely persuaded me that life moves on and that the merry-go-round could not be a stopping place.

Peter, James, and John were so inspired by that breathless moment on Mount Tabor that they wanted to stay there. They would have been content to stop life's parade and settle in on that mountain. But Jesus knew there was human need in the valley and they couldn't stay in the glory on the mountain when there was need in the valley.

Life has many stopping places and we can become imprisoned by them. For some, it may be hard to let go of the past, of old resentments or painful memories. For others it may be lingering bouts with sickness or depression. In the last years of my career, I had the feeling of being trapped, that life was like that merry-go-round—a lot of activity, but no movement.

Stopping places keep us from growing, whether they be old stereotypes, ancient grievances, or present situations. Abraham Maslow said it well. "Every human being has *both* sets of forces within him. One clings to safety and defensiveness out of fear, tending to regress backward, hanging on to the past, afraid to *grow* . . . afraid to take chances. . . . The other set of forces impels him forward toward Wholeness of self, toward full functioning of all his capacities."

The first taste of freedom in this retirement journey has been great. But somehow this cannot be a stopping place in the pilgrimage of faith. Jesus would not let the disciples stay on the mountain, they had to return to the valley where human need awaited them. So it is for the retired Christian. Personal pleasures, new freedom to do as we please, and the inexpressible joy of private time cannot become a mountain where we stay. The call of Christ is always to respond to human need. And so we sing with the writer of "Where Cross the Crowded Ways of Life:"

> Where cross the crowded ways of life,
> Where sound the cries of race and clan,
> Above the noise of selfish strife,
> We hear Thy voice, O Son of Man.

GOD AND FATHER OF JESUS CHRIST:
Lead us to life's stopping places,
but call us to new opportunities for service to others
in the valleys of this world.
AMEN.

16

An Unconventional Life
READ MATTHEW 11:16-19

*These all died in faith,
not having received the promises, but having seen them afar
off were assured of them, embraced them, and confessed that
they were strangers and pilgrims on the earth.
(Hebrews 11:13, NKJV)*

JESUS COMPARED HIS GENERATION to children playing games in the marketplace. "We played the flute for you, and you did not dance; We mourned to you, and you did not lament" (Matthew 11:17, NKJV). Some wanted to play wedding, and others wanted to play funeral, but nothing seemed to please the rest. Crowds went to hear John the Baptist and he didn't dance to their tune. The religious leaders threw their pious religion in Jesus' face and he refused to join their funeral. They even called him "a gluttonous man, and a winebibber, a friend of tax collectors and sinners!" (Matthew 11:19, NKJV).

Christ was unconventional. He shocked his contemporaries with a joyous, free-spirited life style and a kinship with outcasts and outsiders. He refused to be boxed in by the customs and conventions of the time, shocking religious leaders with unaccustomed words and actions.

One of the great enemies of the spirit is routine and convention. We do what others do; we see what others see; we conform to protect ourselves from being rejected or thought different.

Retirement can bring freedom from conventionality because it can bring with it a new freedom to be oneself. One can dispense with all the games, and lay it on the line. One can take more risks and dare to be different. One can suddenly realize how much unnecessary, self-inflicted anxiety was created by worrying about what other people think.

These days, I find myself saying exactly what I feel and often shocking people with my honesty. I no longer have the need to gain the approval of others, nor do I care about being thought different. I saunter down streets wearing an old Yankees cap, and faded jeans. I have even grown a beard.

Some think that this beard means I have embarked on some "old age crisis" or that retirement is so hard that I am hiding behind my beard. They do not realize that the beard represents my newfound freedom to be open, not closed!

Malcom Cowley, at the age of eighty, wrote some powerful words for retirees who dare to be unconventional. Referring to our need to maintain our identity, he says, "It is a fascinating pursuit in itself, and our efforts will not have been wasted if they help us to possess our own identities as an artist possesses his work."

We bring to retirement the person we have become all through the journey of life. I have always marched to a different drummer, but now being unconventional is becoming a new way of life.

UNCONVENTIONAL GOD:
We cannot confine you within our finite limits,
you always are beyond us. Help us to dare to be different
in a world of deadening conformity.
AMEN.

In the Middle of a Muddle
READ GENESIS 11:31–12:4

*Terah took Abram his son and
Lot the son of Haran, his grandson and Sarai, his daughter-in-law . . . and they went forth together from Ur of the
Chaldeans to go into the land of Canaan;
but when they came to Haran, they settled there.
(Genesis 11:31, RSV)*

AS A BOY I ALWAYS LOOKED FORWARD TO the annual visit of the circus and nothing excited me more than watching the trapeze artists. Timing is essential for those artists. In order to get to the next trapeze bar, they first had to let go of the bar they were holding. That surely wasn't easy, for that first bar represented security, and the next bar was the unknown. It seemed like an eternity to me when they did let go and hovered for a breathless moment high above the circus dome. Then I breathed a sigh of relief as they safely grasped the next bar.

Terah and Abram had come to Haran, a sort of half-way house between the old bar of the past, and the next bar of their future. No doubt they experienced the anxiety of the middle, having to let go of their first support and not yet seizing the second. But God called Abram a second time to let go of the bar and move forward, and Abram went, as the Lord had told him.

Paul Tournier wisely wrote, "So there is always in life a place to leave and a new place to find, and in between a zone of hesitation and uncertainty tinged with more or less intense anxiety." I know that feeling, to be caught as in midair, in the middle of a muddle. For years I had known the satisfaction and security of that first bar. Now, it seemed time to let go and grab hold of this new experience and challenge of redirected days. There is a past security to be relinquished before I can find a new security.

There are times I feel like a door, torn off its hinges. I am not ready for a rocking chair, and yet what lies ahead? Like the first Christians, I feel caught between the times–told that the old is gone, but with nothing new come to take its place. I know that in the long run this too will be a growth experience, but for now I feel like those circus performers, swinging on their trapeze high up under the dome of the circus tent.

Yet, there is an excitement about the suspense. A newness and freshness I have never experienced before seems to await, as I watch for the second bar. This is not just a time of anxiety and uncertainty but a moment of new beginnings. In this meantime, the time in the middle, I will embrace life dearly and lift my voice with the writer of "God of Our Life.".

> God of the coming years, through paths unknown
> We follow Thee;
> When we are strong, Lord, leave us not alone;
> Our refuge be.

SHIELD OF ABRAHAM:
As you were with your ancient friend
that you called to leave security for new beginnings,
be with us as we leave the familiar past,
and face the uncertain future.
In this in-between-time, be our support and shield.
AMEN.

Bored Stiff

READ JOHN 5:1-9

One man there had an illness which had lasted for thirty-eight years, and when Jesus saw him lying there and knew he had been in this condition for a long time, he said. "Do you want to be well again?"

(John 5:5–6, JB)

THE MAN AT THE POOL OF BETHESDA must have been one of the loneliest men in town. An invalid for thirty-eight years, he had hoped to find a cure in the bubbling waters of this pool. Apparently the pool was thought to possess miraculous healing powers. There was a legend that when an angel troubled the waters, the first to get into the pool would be healed of an infirmity.

Jesus asked a question of this man. He knew the man was a malingerer, someone who pretended that he wanted to be well, but in fact preferred illness to health. Jesus then confronted him with a challenge. "Do you want to be well again? . . . Get up! Pick up your sleeping mat and walk." And the man did, just like that. He was healed, a gift of grace from the Great Physician. His paralysis ended, his life began again.

In the early days of retirement, I can feel a kinship with that man at the pool called Bethesda. There are days when I feel immobilized.

I've enjoyed the respite from the rat race but I confess I am becoming bored. The "everybody-seems-to-be-busy-but-me" syndrome is getting to me. I am blessed with a wonderful wife but she still has her demanding career to attend to. And I confess there are times when I envy the neighbors driving off to work in the morning. There are days when there seems to be no purpose to my getting up in the morning.

The problem is not that my life is without things to do or places to go. My days are full but unfulfilled. The paradox is that I am busy and bored at the same time. During my career, there were goals that motivated me. Now the days seem too much the same, and I wonder if I make a difference anymore to anyone. I think words Job's words as he yearned for his former life:

> How I long for the months gone by,
> for the days when God watched over me,
> when his lamp shone upon my head
> and by his light I walked through darkness!
> Oh, for the days when I was in my prime. . . .
> –Job 29:2-4, NIV

I admit that it is all too easy in retirement to become bored stiff. Jesus' words to the man at the pool become a word for all who experience this retirement boredom. "Get up! Pick up your sleeping mat, and walk!" I refuse to torture myself with nostalgic thoughts of the past when I was more active and more goal-oriented. I will decide what I can do in the present.

GOD OF MANY DELIVERANCES:
You have pulled me out of many hard places by your grace.
Help me now to find new ways to make my life count
for the Kingdom.
AMEN.

III

FRAGMENTED BY BUSYNESS

You will get bored and bitter
unless you find something that gives meaning to life
because your need for human dignity
will not settle for less.
Since mere divertissement and distractions
are not enough, a second career will have to grow
from your talents, resources, and interests. . . .
You are an artist whose work is to create yourself
right up to the end.
No one has a right to say when that work is done—
that's God's privilege.

EDWARD FISCHER

My Hat Is Still Missing

READ 1 KINGS 20:35-43

And as your servant was busy here and there, he was gone.
The king of Israel said to him, "So shall your judgment be;
you yourself have decided it."
(1 Kings 20:40, RSV)

IT WAS A HECTIC DAY, one I never expected in my slowed down retirement life. I allowed myself to become a victim of the volunteer trap. I am still a product of the Puritan work ethic, prone to feel guilty if I have too much free time. So I answered many calls from community causes and became over-involved.

The day began with a called meeting of a soup kitchen committee, meeting the crisis of relocating this needed ministry to the hungry. The council on aging followed, and then the aging advisory committee, concerned with transportation and housing needs of the elderly. I ran from meeting to meeting. It was appropriate that the day ended with a meeting to preserve a Chapel of the Rest.

In all that rushing around, I lost my hat. I retraced my steps and still couldn't find it. What a parable of the retirement life. We can become so wrapped up in volunteer work, so busy wearing so many hats, that we lose our perspective, if not our souls.

The servant in the story from the Book of Kings had an important responsibility: to guard the prisoner for the king. But he "became busy here and there," doing many things, and neglected the major thing. He majored in the minors. His intentions were good but other things, not wrong in themselves, got in the way.

All of my own activity had begun to throw me back again into the distress of an overactive life. So I decided to resign from some of those committees and protect my intentions for a redirected life, not allowing myself to fall too far back into the same stress trap from former days. B.F. Skinner and M. E. Vaughn said it well, "Keeping busy does not mean never resting. To rest is not to be bored. It is, rather, one of the most enjoyable things we can do—provided we need it."

I needed that rest. I have to learn to say no to other calls. My self esteem no longer depends on being someone's savior. There are times when someone calls with a worthy cause and I must decline. When the caller seems taken back at my refusal to "serve," I almost want to say, "Pardon me for retiring."

I am working hard in these days not to let myself ever again get trapped in the dizzy whirl of volunteer work. After all, didn't Jesus say, "What, then, will a man gain if he wins the whole world and ruins his life?" (Matthew 16:26, JB).

I still haven't found the missing hat. In fact, I have given up looking for it. It seems to symbolize a second retirement—from full-time volunteer work.

ETERNAL KEEPER:
You have given us the fragile gift of life,
and yet we so often abuse it with our frantic busyness.
Teach us to value this new freedom of retirement, and keep us
from ruining our lives with distressful activities.
AMEN.

20

Crushed by Committees
READ ECCLESIASTES 2:17-23

What does a man get for all the toil and anxious striving
with which he labors under the sun? All his days his work is
pain and grief; even at night his mind does not rest.
This too is meaningless.
(Ecclesiastes 2:22–23, NIV)

RECENTLY I READ ABOUT A MAN who invented a beeper
that could be set off at any moment. If he was trapped
in a boring meeting or a dull committee session, he
could set off the beeper and make a gracious exit.
People would not realize he was leaving because of
boredom but would assume he was off on some
important errand. There are times when I wish I
possessed such a beeper. It may be too severe to concur
with the comic who called committees, "a group of the
unqualified, appointed by the unwilling, to do the
unnecessary." Committees can be productive. But they
can also be terribly tedious and time consuming.

The Book of Ecclesiastes is a bit like a random
collection of an old college professor's notes on his
assessment of the meaning of life. Koheleth sought
meaning in knowledge, pleasure, wealth, and work,
and discovered, "all is vanity, and a striving after
wind." He realizes that all our projects, meetings and
ventures cannot give ultimate meaning. And,
furthermore, the distress that work brings causes
vexation and sleepless nights.

I recall so many times in my former days at work when I became frustrated with non-productive meetings. Even then, I often echoed the prayer of Psalm 55:

O that I had wings like a dove!
I would fly away and be at rest;
yea, I would wander afar,
I would lodge in the wilderness,
I would haste to find me a shelter
from the raging wind and tempest.
–Psalm 55:6–8, RSV

Now, time is even more precious to me, as an older person has no guarantee of how much time is left. At a busy clinic in a retirement community, one of the newest doctors on staff suggested that walk-in patients be given a number, so that they could be called by number. The harried receptionist complied at first but later refused to continue the practice. When asked the reason, she called the doctor to the waiting room window. "Look out there." she said as she pointed at all the older patients. "Would *you* want to tell one of those people their number is up?"

Time is precious in retirement years and does not need to be frittered away in non-productive meetings. There is a place for vital, productive committee meetings. But I have reached the time in life that I will speak up when meetings deteriorate into trivialities or lose perspective. One day, I may even get a beeper and get up and walk out in protest!

CREATOR OF ALL:
*Give us the patience to endure what cannot be
changed and courage to change what needs to be changed.
Deliver us from meetings that crush our spirits.*
AMEN.

21

Distracted by Busyness
READ LUKE 10:38-42

"Martha, Martha," he said,
"you worry and fret about so many things, and yet
few are needed, indeed only one."
(Luke 10:41, JB)

MARTHA HAD A BIG JOB. Hospitality was of no small importance to the Jewish people, and the women of the household were expected to entertain their guests with refreshment and tend to their needs. On this day, Jesus was to be the honored guest, and Martha no doubt wanted the occasion to be a special one. No wonder that when the Master arrived, she became out of sorts with her younger sister Mary. "Lord, do you not care that my sister is leaving me to do the serving all by myself? Please tell her to help me" (Luke 10:40, JB). Our hearts go out to Martha.

Jesus lovingly rebukes Martha and affirms Mary, who quietly sits at his feet and listens. Mary is doing the unprecedented: she is sitting at the feet of Jesus, in the company of the men, and receiving his teaching. As women were not permitted to be instructed in the Law, Mary's actions were a distinct break with Jewish tradition. Jesus encouraged her and reminded Martha that her sister had made the better choice.

Let's be clear. Jesus did not scold Martha for being a hostess, nor would he dismiss the kitchen as a place for experiencing God's presence. He was concerned that she was distracted by her serving. She was missing the divine moment. She was letting activity be more important than relationships.

I can easily identify with Martha's distraction. So many good causes, so much need. All of this busyness has its place but it can detract from single-minded love of God. Martha fell into the "servant snare"–becoming so preoccupied with her servant role that she lost the moment with the Master. Mary took time to be present with Jesus, to not let necessary tasks deprive her of a spiritual feast. Her relationship with Jesus was more important than much serving.

I now have a rich opportunity to deepen my spiritual life. I am not bound any longer by the constraints of a full-time job or the demands of others. But in these early days of retirement, I am getting distracted by all this busy work. I don't need to bustle around, offering unneeded advice or help. I am humbled by how well things go without me. What I need now is to choose Mary's way. What I need now is more time cultivating the spiritual life with more focus on a life of unceasing prayer. The words of Thomas R. Kelly speak to my condition, "One can live in a well-nigh continuous state of unworded prayer, directed toward God, directed toward people and enterprises we have on our heart . . . it is a life unspeakable and full of glory, an inner world of splendor." I must not let anything distract me from this.

LOVER OF SOULS:
You seek us even when we become distracted
by life's demands. Help us to know that this life is
meaningless without your presence.
AMEN.

22

Watch Out for the Empty House
READ MATTHEW 12:43-45

But on arrival, find it unoccupied, swept and tidied,
it then goes off and collects seven other spirits more evil than
itself, and they go in and set up house there, so that the man
ends up by being worse than he was before.
(Matthew 12:45, JB)

"THE MAN ENDS UP BY BEING worse than he was before,"
said Jesus. That is the punch line of the story. The devil
had departed but returned to the house from which he
had been expelled and finds it in better shape than
when he left it. His erstwhile landlord had been doing
some fall cleaning. He had redecorated the whole place.
It was swept clean but it was empty. So the tired devil
returned and brought seven other spirits more evil than
himself.

The man's house of life was swept and polished–it
was clean and beautiful. But even a clean and well
decorated life, if it is also empty, creates room for
devils. Jesus is warning that the empty house is also an
invitation to devils and that unless we replace evil with
good, the change may pave the way for greater evils
than they displaced.

Since I retired, I have tried to "put my house in
order." Priorities have been established, some volunteer
work undertaken in the community, and ample time set
aside for my own needs. But there is still an emptiness
that bothers me.

There are times when I feel that the retired life can become so self-centered that my major concern seems to be my own peace of mind and comfort. Although I feel good about purging my house of some evil spirits–addiction to work, distress and burn-out–I question whether any positive goals or reasons for being have replaced them. I am reminded of the words of Fosdick's hymn "God of Grace and God of Glory":

> Shame our wanton, selfish gladness,
> Rich in things and poor in soul.
> Grant us wisdom, grant us courage,
> Lest we miss thy Kingdom's goal.

Busyness is not the answer, but then neither is this emptiness. God said to Joshua in his later years, "You are very old, but there is still much land to be taken" (Joshua 13:1, TEV). Living a clean life, minding my own business, and sweeping my house clean of old ghosts still leaves it empty. So, the search must continue for God's will, for some mission, for some kingdom goal that will bring meaning to these years.

Richard Bach says, "Here is a test to find whether your mission on earth is finished: If you're alive, it isn't." Well, I'm alive, but I still haven't found that mission.

ANSWER TO ALL MYSTERIES:
Teach us patience when we cannot
see the way ahead. Deliver us from emptiness of life
and fill us with your purpose.
AMEN.

23

Playing Antique Bingo
READ EPHESIANS 5:15-20

*See then that you walk circumspectly,
not as fools but as wise, redeeming the time,
because the days are evil.*
(Ephesians 5:15–16, NKJV)

WE DO ALL KINDS OF THINGS TO TIME: We use it, waste it, mark it, kill it, and make it. Some unfortunate people even "do" time. One of the less talked about manifestations of retirement is the fear of free time.

Jane Thibault tells a story about "Catherine," an affluent, sixty-seven year-old widow of a physician who expressed the void in her life this way. "I'm playing 'antique bingo'–the way other people play real bingo–just to kill time amusing myself." Antique bingo. I've played that game, too,.

Since I retired, I've tried to kill some time myself by amusing myself with all kinds of pastimes. I've cleaned out my files, catalogued all the books in my library, worked on my photography, spent quality time with grandchildren, and even worked in the garden. I've enjoyed some of it but I have to admit much of it has been playing antique bingo.

Fear of free time prevents some people from even considering retirement. I spoke last week with a sixty-two year old friend who frankly admitted he would *not* retire until they carried him out, since he had never developed any other interests except his work and would be petrified by the free time. Others who do retire find their newfound freedom marred by this overabundance of time. A few weeks of rest and relaxation cleanses us from exhaustion, and then we are eager for some new plateau. But there often seems nothing to go on to.

Paul cautions the Ephesians to redeem the time. That word means the same thing that it meant in Galatians when God said, "In the fullness of time, I sent my son to *redeem* those who were under the law." We are to live redemptively, as instruments of God's purpose, to redeem *this* time. Rather than frittering away time in retirement, even this time must be redeemed for God's purposes.

So Paul goes on to say, "Therefore, do not be foolish, but understand what the will of the Lord is" (Ephesians 5:17, NKJV). The word foolish means to act rashly without reflection, to be senseless. At any age, we redeem the time when we are fulfilling God's purpose for our growth in his image, whatever we happen to be doing.

It felt good to play some antique bingo, but I am not sure that it was also redeeming the time. Stepping off the treadmill of work has helped me learn to play. But I am sure there is something more that God wants us to be and do when we retire other than chase our own pursuits.

REDEEMING GOD:

Teach us to redeem our time, to use this day for some purpose that goes beyond our own needs and interests.

AMEN.

24

That Dislocated Feeling
READ PSALM 73

But as for me; my feet had almost slipped;
I had nearly lost my foothold.
(Psalm 73:2, NIV)

ONE OF THE STRONG FEELINGS I've experienced in these days is one of being dislocated, as if life didn't include me anymore, that I didn't belong. Jules Z. Willing said that "the unanswered question is not so much what happens *to* people when they retire as what happens *in* people when they retire. As long as this question remains unanswered . . . each of us must experience retirement as though we were the first to enter it."

I think this is true of a lot of retired persons. Being dislocated is not just a matter of moving to a retirement community or a smaller house. It is a state of the soul. Walter Brueggemann writes that the Psalms point to the fact that our life of faith consists in moving with God in terms of being securely oriented, painfully disoriented, and surprisingly reoriented. Moving from security into dislocation brings negative feelings. When we move to a new orientation, we are surprised by God's new gift. Amazement and thanksgiving ensue.

My joy at being freed from the chaos of the workday world is being replaced by a feeling of being dislocated, unsure of what the future holds. My old, familiar world is gone, the new world has yet to be found.

Robert Atchley names six retirement stages: pre-retirement, honeymoon, disenchantment, reorientation, stability, and termination. I am somewhere between disenchantment and reorientation, struggling with this new stage in life.

The psalmist experienced this dislocation. A crisis overwhelms him and he feels he has lost his foothold. He questions whether his faithfulness has been a waste of time, especially when he sees the prosperity of the wicked. It is only when he goes to the sanctuary of God that his faith returns. He discovers that whatever happens, the main thing is God's loving presence. "Yet I am always with you; you hold me by my right hand. You guide me with your counsel, and afterward you will take me into glory" (Psalm 73:23–24, NIV).

Every day I reaffirm the importance of worship in God's sanctuary and prayer in the inner sanctuary. I see no answers yet. The feeling of being in limbo remains. But moments of worship and prayer reassure me of the presence of that Holy Mystery that is my greatest joy.

Kathleen Fischer tells of a student whose father had been depressed since retirement. The son realized the family had done nothing to mark the event. At supper, each member of the family brought two symbols: something they were grateful for that was the result of their father's working years and a symbol of hope for his future. One son brought his college diploma and thanked his father for providing for his education.

What intrigues me about the story is the second symbol: hope for the future. Disorientation will come; it may even seem like the times have gone crazy. Some assurance that there is a future, that God will bring a new gift into our lives, would be a blessing.

SUSTAINER OF LIFE:
We thank you for your constant presence to us in times of
confusion, darkness, and uncertainty.
AMEN.

25

Am I Wasting What's Left?
READ MARK 14:3-10

But there were some who said to themselves indignantly,
"Why was this ointment thus wasted?"
(Mark 14:4, RSV)

I SPENT SEVERAL HOURS VISITING FRIENDS at a retirement community. They seemed quite active as they rushed from one activity to the next. Two things bothered me: Retirement communities can fall into the trap of fostering a kind of geriatric segregation, where older people are deprived of contact with the younger generation; and, all this frenetic activity we associate with retirement can become a terrible waste.

When the woman at Bethany broke open the expensive alabaster jar of ointment and anointed Jesus there were some who said indignantly, "Why this waste?" Why indeed? It seemed a foolish thing to do. That perfume was very precious; Mark's Gospel tells us it was worth a whole year's wages. Think of what that might have done for the poor in Jerusalem. But Jesus rallies to her defense, and calls her act a "lovely deed," whereby she was the first to anoint his body, in anticipation of his sacrifice. It was a lovely, creative waste that time would never tarnish. Wherever in all the world the gospel is preached, this "waste" will become her memorial.

We live in a disposable, plastic society that fosters destructive waste. Sometimes people waste lives with addictions to alcohol or drugs. But this was a creative waste as this woman who perceived Jesus' true identity, offered a work of love, which cost her dearly.

In that same retirement community, I met a woman in her eighties who did not allow herself to be caught up in all the frantic activities of that place. She gave some of her time every day to read stories to children in a daycare center. The children came from wasted homes; they were unhealed victims of violence and addictions. Some might call her time "wasted" and yet, like the woman at Bethany, it is a waste of love.

As I drove home that afternoon, I asked myself the question, "Am I wasting what's left of my life?" Retirement is not a license to be free from ministry. In this redirected life, where can I find a place where I can break open the alabaster jar and anoint others with grace in his name?

I pondered the meaning of this story and how its real meaning is found only at the cross. The cross is the supreme example of God's extravagant love for us. In many ways it all seemed such a foolish waste. Jesus was such a young man, with so much more to do and to say and to be. "Why this waste?" Through Christ's poured out blood and his broken body, God's extravagant love redeemed the world.

MIGHTY REDEEMER:
We pause to recognize your outlandish love for us.
In these days when we can find time to waste for others,
direct us to some place of service.
AMEN.

26

Carpe Diem
READ MATTHEW 6:25-34

*This is the day that the Lord had made;
let us rejoice and be glad in it.
(Psalm 118:24, NRSV)*

HOW MANY PEOPLE ASK THE SAME QUESTION: "What will I do when I am retired?"

"For once, I'm going to do exactly as I please."
"My aging parents need more and more care, so I'm retiring to take care of them."
"I've retired to do all those things I never had time to do when I was working."
"I'm just going to exist. All my life I've taken care of others; now it's their turn to take care of me."

Early in retirement there are so many options that at times I become bewildered at all this new freedom. Time becomes more precious every day, for it is hard to escape the haunting reality that life is winding down.

Kathleen Fischer says, "But there is a sense in which we can speak of the period of Jesus' public ministry as his later years. Christians have puzzled for generations over the length of time given to Jesus' hidden life, thirty years or so, in contrast to the brief period allotted to the more important tasks of preaching, teaching, working miracles, and shaping a group of disciples. . . . No time is too short for the purposes of God. Jesus' last years numbered only three; for many older persons today, the later years number more like twenty-five to thirty."

Later years are full of new possibilities and we must, as the Latin phrase *carpe diem* says, seize the day and not fritter away what may well be the most significant years of our lives. "*This* is the day the Lord has made."

Working with some residents in a long term care center, I found them slow to respond to questions, so I asked them a simple one: "Can you name two days of the week that begin with the letter T ?" One gentleman quickly replied, "Today and tomorrow." What wisdom. Today is all we have. Tomorrow is God's extra bonus.

I still struggle with the distractions and demands on my "free" time. Causes clamor for my help; I find myself giving in to temptations to crowd my calendar and busily planning the future. I need to *carpe diem*.

A tradition in ancient China called for two calendars to mark the life of each person. One was kept from birth and noted events up through age sixty. A second one was presented on the sixty-first birthday. The second calendar was called *Kanreki*–the second childhood.

That is what seizing the day really means. A second childhood for finding beauty in God's world, enjoying family and friends, forming new relationships, taking new risks, realizing we are responsible only to ourselves and to God.

I know a lady who taught school for fifty years and then retired. Each day she takes time to cheer someone or bring encouragement to an older person. She seizes the day. On one occasion, she gave me the prayer of the old fisherman which I now pray almost every day, "O Lord the sea is so great–and my boat is so small."

GOD OF THIS DAY

We get so distracted during these days of retirement that we miss golden opportunities for seeing beauty and enjoying life. Teach us to make this day a moment of glory.
AMEN.

27

Neither Rust Nor Rush
READ MATTHEW 6:19-21

But store up for yourselves treasures in heaven,
where moth and rust do not destroy, and where thieves do not
break in and steal. For where your treasure is,
there will be your heart also.
(Matthew 6:20–21, NIV)

IT SEEMS THAT ALREADY I have experienced two of the most subtle dangers anyone faces in the redirected life. I began this journey in constant fear that I would "rust out." I had approached "burn-out" in my life as pastor-in-charge, but as I withdrew I wondered if I would just fade into oblivion. It seemed as if Maggie Kuhn's concern that older people be considered scrap and surplus might be all too true.

When I attended my first presbytery meeting after retirement, I discovered my name had been stricken from the active role, as if the power structure considered me "out of it." Because I was no longer a pastor-in-charge, I felt I had become a non-person, relegated to the scrap heap, considered expendable, someone whose primary role was to give way to the "younger" clergy. I asserted myself and let them know that despite retirement, I was still available and usable.

So I plunged headlong into busy activities in the community and church. One of the clichés I used with friends was "I am still looking for all that time I'm supposed to have in retirement." I see that now as a defense mechanism to protect my need to kill time out of boredom and fear of abandonment. Then some words from Frederick Buechner spoke to my condition. "The world is full of people who in one way or another are by and large merely 'getting through' their lives, who are killing their time, who are living so much on the surface of things . . . that it is little wonder that one life seems enough to them or more than enough."

I realized that so much of my rushing about was just killing time, and made little sense. I knew that retirement life is busy but I refused to let it crowd out my sense of who I am or where I am going. Perhaps the joke about people who retired to a hilltop home in South Dakota and named it Mount Rush-No-More has more truth than we admit.

So I am pulling back from the endless hustle and bustle. I lose some ego strokes that come from others' approval but I am finding a new sense of centeredness and peace. I realized there is another four-letter word for retirees which does have merit: rest. The ancient prophet warned the ancient Israelites, "In repentance and rest is your salvation, in quietness and trust is your strength, but you would have none of it" (Isaiah 30:15, NIV). But I have learned through my experience. From now on, it is neither rust nor rush, but rest.

CREATOR AND PRESERVER OF ALL HUMANKIND:
Thank you for showing us a better way.
We have allowed ourselves to be distracted from you.
Preserve us from busyness and from uselessness.
AMEN.

IV

DOWNUM STREET BLUES

*The moment of retirement itself
may be a shocking encounter with the transition
about to be made. . . . For the unprepared,
for those whose creativity and involvement in work
has been of major importance and whose identity is
largely derived from that work,
there can be a bitter and deprived feeling
of being expelled and depreciated.*

ERIK H. ERIKSON, JOAN M. ERICKSON
and HELEN Q. KIVNICK

28

Downnum Street Blues
READ PSALM 42

Why are you cast down, O my soul,
and why are you disquieted within me? Hope in God;
for I shall again praise him, my help and my God.
(Psalm 42:11, RSV)

IT WAS A DEPRESSING DAY. The phone doesn't ring that much anymore and I feel as though I have been discarded, like a piece of old furniture. People seem so preoccupied with their own issues, and I miss the social contacts of work and valued friends. I miss my congregation, the people whose lives touched mine, but who are now out of sight.

I decided to try and walk off my depression instead of wallowing in my self-pity. As I trudged through the empty streets, I happened to glance at a street sign and it said Downum Street. How appropriate for a retired person. When one leaves the world of work with its stimulation and affirmations, one will walk quite often on "Downum Street."

Patrick J. Brennan says that the three components of depression are anger, loss, and lacking. I began to realize how very real were my losses–loss of work, loss of friends, loss of identity. How would I introduce myself now that I could no longer claim a work identity? Should I mention my past work, or just say, "I'm retired."

Retired! The word sounds so final. My retirement ceremony felt more like a funeral. I know that Freud said that we shelve death, try to hush it up, and that everyone is convinced of their own immortality in their unconscious. However, retirement makes one think about one's demise. I know now how the old psalmist felt when he prayed to God, "Do not reject me now I am old, nor desert me now my strength is falling. . . . Now that I am old and grey, God, do not desert me." (Psalm 71:9, 18, JB) It is no wonder that so many people refuse to plan for retirement and can't imagine what it will be like to be without a job. No wonder they won't even think about it. In retirement, I still have plans but now life no longer seems endless.

All the same, I began to sense once again that irresistible grace that had surrounded my life. Paul's words come back to me–"By the grace of God, I am what I am" (1 Corinthians 15:10, RSV). I can affirm my life and recognize that my worth does not depend on my work, but on the grace and love of God. We are justified by faith.

My depression began to lift. I knew, too well, that there would be other dark nights. But at least I had gotten in touch with my depression and began to realize how much grief I had experienced in the loss of work and identity. For now, I was grateful for the present. With Dag Hammarskjöld I could now affirm, "–Night is drawing nigh–/For all that has been–Thanks!/ To all that shall be–Yes!"

I had walked up Downum Street.

GIVER OF HEALTH AND SALVATION:
You know our feeble frames, fearful hearts, and anxious minds. Help us to so lean on your everlasting arms that nothing can ever get us down.
AMEN.

29

From Who's Who to Who's That?

READ JOB 29

Oh, for the days when I was in my prime.
(Job 29:4, NIV)

A HIGHLY SUCCESSFUL BANKER decided to retire at fifty-five and arranged all his affairs so as to insure a secure future. He even arranged for part-time work as a consultant to non-profit organizations. But some of his apprehension about this major transition was expressed in some words he shared with me, "At times I feel like I may go from *Who's Who* to *Who's That*?"

Retirement may open to a new sense of freedom but it can also close the book on your former sense of identity. Robert L. Veninga notes that, "while some adults move into retirement without missing a beat in their busy lives, many do not. In fact most . . . told me that it took them from one to three years to fully come to grips with what it meant to be retired."

The patriarch Job, who may well have been in *Who's Who* list in the land of Uz, suddenly plummets to the depths of depression. He recalls the days when he was "the chief, the king among troops," the leader among leaders. He remembers those better days when his counsel was revered and his name synonymous with justice and compassion. He years for the days when he was in his prime. His lament is not just over the loss of bygone days but the loss of God's blessing as well.

Nathan Billig has said, "Depression in the older adult is complex and involves the biology of aging, the mixture of losses and successes throughout life, the interplay of medical illnesses and their treatments, and the strengths and weaknesses that make up the person." Some of the empty feeling that comes with retirement is the loss of one's career identity. "Oh, for the days when I was in my prime."

Billig adds, "Depression is surely something with which many older adults must contend. It is not just sadness. It is a clinical problem. . . . Up to 15 to 20% of older people are depressed. Most of these suffer in silence, and remain undiagnosed, misdiagnosed, and most importantly, untreated."

How did Job deal with his depression? By not surrendering his integrity. "Till I die, I will not deny my integrity," he asserts to his friend, Bildad (Job 27:5, NIV). He could not understand the ways of God in his life but he would not surrender to despair.

Noted psychoanalyst Erik Erikson views old age as the stage of life that involves a struggle of ego integrity versus despair. When one accepts his or her life, feels good about it and would not live it over, later life can be faced with integrity. Integrity gives a basis for approaching the end of life with the feeling of having lived completely.

When we are tempted to become depressed about being out of the limelight and no longer needed as in former days, we can affirm our life with integrity and find new joy in a simpler life, with its precious time now available for family, friends, and second careers.

GOD OF COMFORT:
You understand our weaknesses and take pride in our strengths. When we feel at a loss because of losing our status or stimulation, create new opportunities for us that will give us hope.
AMEN.

30

Flat Tired
READ HEBREWS 10:32-39

A bruised reed he will not break,
and a dimly burning wick he will not quench.
(Isaiah 42:3, RSV)

ONE OF THE INEVITABLE LOSSES that goes with older age is the loss of energy. There are some days when you feel depleted, as if all the air is gone–flat tired. One of my retired friends told me that he had difficulty getting up in the morning, because he felt there were no projects or creative work to motivate him. "I wanted to retire to get some relief from the distress at work, and it was time. But I've run out of things to do, and now I'm just immobile."

I have witnessed too many retirees who withdraw from life and surrender to the "given up/giving in" syndrome. The depression causes feelings of helplessness and hopelessness.

It seems to me that some of our malaise in retirement is not physical burnout but rather it is spiritual burnout. It is certainly true that any serious believer goes through times when he or she feels like a dimly burning wick. Life seems to spin along without any meaning or future. It is at these moments that faith becomes real.

The early Hebrew Christians had been through difficult times. In the midst of those hard times they were tempted to waver and were in danger of losing "the great reward." The years had rolled on, and they had grown weary in the Christian way. Perhaps they felt a let-down and now suffered from tired blood.

The author exhorts them: "Don't give up. Don't drift away. Hold fast in faith to the Christian tradition. Do not throw away your confidence, which has a great reward. You need endurance." If they would keep faith, they would keep their souls.

It may be that I have been so busy, so distracted by other things, that I have not practiced the presence of God. It is time "to rest beside the weary road, and hear the angels sing." One consolation is that a tired and disillusioned heart is closer to God than a happy one. Did not Jesus say "Come to Me, all you who labor and are heavy laden, and I will give you rest"? (Matthew 11:28, NKJV).

Can it be that now—when my burned out life no longer finds the least bit of joy in things that formerly gave me relief, when even the pastimes and pleasures of my ordinary life that I used to call upon to help me over this emptiness no longer satisfy—that I can find the true rest?

SOURCE OF HEALTH AND STRENGTH:
You understand our weariness and loss of energy.
Help us to turn to you and to find help in your grace
in our time of need.
AMEN.

31

Unfinished Grief Work
READ PSALM 137

By the waters of Babylon,
there we sat down and wept, when we remembered Zion.
On the willows there we hung up our lyres.
(Psalm 137: 1–2, RSV)

THE DISPLACED HEBREWS were still locked in their grief. When their captors demanded that they sing one of their songs of Zion, there was no way they could comply. (Especially since they had put their musical instruments in mothballs!) Grief over the loss of the Temple in Jerusalem gave them little heart for music.

I now realize that some of my depression and lack of energy in this time is due to unfinished grief work over my loss of full-time work. Unresolved grief brings a sense of paralysis and loss of energy. Grieving people withdraw from life and seem immobilized. Often they handle depression with too much sleeping and TV.

Scott Sullender clearly shows the major loss that occurs at retirement when he writes,

> Most of us invest ourselves in our jobs. They are . . . activities that we feel reflect on us and give our lives meaning. . . . So it is, then, that one of the major losses in the later years is the loss of work. . . .Eventually, we must give up our work and all the feelings of worthiness, identity and productivity that go with it.

The captors' taunts shocked them from their lethargy and started a new train of thought. "If I forget you, O

Jerusalem, let my right hand wither!" (Psalm 137:5, RSV). Happy memories of past years in Jerusalem filled their hearts, and their grief was transformed into anger against their enemies and resolve to begin again in these new surroundings.

Retirement does demand constant grief work over the loss of work. But we do have time to slow down and reflect, to not be afraid to look inward or go deeper. We hallow memories of happy days at our Jerusalems and we pray our good-byes. Then it is time to gather our resources and move on. King David grieved for seven days for the young child of Bathsheba who lay near death. When David heard the news that the child had died, his biographer tells us, "Then David arose from the earth, and washed, and anointed himself, and changed his clothes; and he went into the house of the LORD and worshipped" (2 Samuel 12:20, RSV).

So I have begun to work through my grief with symbolic acts–refusing to answer calls for help from my former parish, finding new interests, meeting new friends.

It is important to grieve the loss of full-time work, for so much of ourselves has been wrapped up in it. But there comes a time when it is time to move on with life.

COMFORT OF SUFFERERS:
Sometimes we like to give the impression
that we are overjoyed to be retired and free from work.
Yet, we do feel a deep loss of esteem, recognition, and friends.
Help us to work through this grief to growth.
AMEN.

32

The Bent-Over Woman
READ LUKE 13:10–17

For you, O LORD, have delivered my soul from death,
my eyes from tears, my feet from stumbling,
that I may walk before the LORD in the land of the living.
(Psalm 116:8–9, NIV)

SHE RETIRED A FEW YEARS AGO, after teaching many years. She and her husband planned to enjoy their retirement and then came the dreadful news: He was suffering from incurable cancer. After he died, she lost interest in life and withdrew. She told me, "When he died, my life ended, too. So I drew the blinds around the windows of my life and, except for going to church on Sunday, I became a recluse." She reluctantly came to our life review group but remained locked in despair.

I had never reflected on the story of the bent-over women in Luke's Gospel until someone asked me to open my Bible to the thirteenth chapter of Luke, and there she was, the bent-over woman. The story begins with Jesus teaching in the synagogue, and he sees a woman who is bent over and unable to straighten up. The text does not tell us why she's bent over, but it does say that she's been that way for eighteen years. That's a long time for her to bear her infirmity and pain.

Why was she bent over? Perhaps it came from picking up her husband's and children's clothes for eighteen years. Or, in that male dominated society, her predicament may have been caused by being put down every time she tried to be somebody. It might have been that her work as a slave caused her predicament.

One of the meanings of the word *infirmity* is spiritual weakness. We cannot begin to know what stress, what emotional burdens, what debilitating problems the woman carried on her back. But Jesus said to her, "Woman, you are freed from your infirmity. And he immediately laid his hands upon her, and immediately she was made straight" (Luke 13:12–13, RSV). In Christ, she found the liberating power to walk tall.

The "bent-over" woman in our group changed, too. As the group listened to her story, shared her pain, and responded to her need, she realized that her husband's death was not the end of her life. She found affirmation from a group of Christians who gave her the precious gifts of empathy and acceptance. One group member told her, "I have never been in your classroom, nor did I know your husband. But I really like you as you are now." She walked out of the room with a new look on her face and her head held high. We all felt her retirement would be different from that day on.

> Down in the human heart, Crushed by the tempter,
> Feelings lie buried that grace can restore;
> Touched by a loving heart, Wakened by kindness,
> Chords that are broken will vibrate once more.
> *–From "Rescue the Perishing"*

STRENGTH OF THE WEAK:
It is so easy to give up in these latter days of life, especially when we lose a loved one or feel unwanted. Strengthen us, that we may stand straight and walk with courage and hope.
AMEN.

33

The Ever-present Threat
READ PSALM 38

Remember your Creator in the days of your youth,
before the days of trouble come, and the years approach
when you will say, "I find no pleasure in them."
(Ecclesiastes 12:1, NIV)

I VISITED A FRIEND WHO had retired several years ago. He was having to undergo unexpected surgery. He looked at me and said, "At our age, you never know what threat will come knocking at your door."

Days later, sitting in a doctor's office, I awaited word about some medical tests of my own. Threats to your health become more present and possible when you reach the Third Age. Before trouble comes, indeed!

In the fourth century B.C., Damocles was enjoying the grandeur and delights of a luxurious banquet. His attention was directed upwards. He saw a sharp sword hanging above him by a single horsehair. The sword of Damocles hangs over our heads as well. We never know what the day may bring.

One of the great fears of older age is the fear of losing control, of not being able to cope. Maybe that's why we don't like to be away from home. It may explain why we dislike dealing with situations that seem to threaten our personal security. Often, we worry most about things that never happen. But I never find it helpful to be told not to worry. Even if the crisis passes and what I fear *doesn't* happen, the worry remains that the threat will be back. Only older persons can understand.

My friend survived the surgery and I got a good test result. But even then I couldn't shrug off the feeling that some "pestilence that stalks in the darkness" or "plague that destroys at midday" (Psalm 91:6, NIV) still threatened my life.

I always liked what Frederick Buechner says about imaginary terminal illnesses in *A Room Called Remember.*

> There is something to be said for such nonsense. For one thing, to have the doctor tell you that it is not lung cancer after all . . . is in a way to be born again. . . . it is to be given back not just your old life again but your old life with a new sense of its pricelessness.

How true. When one gets a good report, and the sword doesn't descend after all, one feels re-energized, and cherishes this gift we call life. But the fear remains. Each day seems to demand a constant vigilance against dangers and threats.

Dr. Luke, the compassionate physician, must have understood these feelings. Only in Luke's Gospel do we find Simeon saying, "And a sword will pierce your own soul too" (Luke 2:35, NIV). He was saying to Mary that her joy at the birth of her son must be tempered by the ever-present sword of threat.

So in the midst of threat, under the ever-present sword, we cling to the love of God and believe that "We are hard pressed on every side, but not crushed; perplexed, but not in despair" (2 Corinthians 4:8, NIV).

GOD OF COMPASSION:
You know our weakness, our fears, and our inability to trust.
Forgive us. May we find strength in your presence,
where nothing can separate us from your love.
AMEN.

34

Healing Our Memories
READ PSALM 103

They made me keeper of the vineyards; but,
my own vineyard I have not kept!
(Song of Solomon 1:6, RSV)

As far as the east is from the west,
so far does he remove our transgressions from us.
(Psalm 103:12, RSV)

WRITING OR RECORDING OUR LIFE STORIES is a gift for the next generation, especially in this age with more distance between families. We all have a story to tell, and unless we hand it on to the next generation, we may become a nameless face, a person whose story is lost forever. Retirement provides a golden opportunity for such reflection. And so, I have begun the time consuming task of changing memories into memoirs.

Recalling my past made me depressed. Perhaps part of it had to do with facing my own mortality. The longer you live, the closer you are to death, and there seemed to be something so final about writing memoirs.

More reflection helped me get in touch with the sources of my depression. In my earlier life, I was so preoccupied with my career, and had such a burning drive to succeed that there was little time left for my children. Those magical years are soon gone. When your children are little, you wonder if they are ever going to grow up. When they are grown, you stand amazed at what happened to those childhood years.

In those earlier years, I tried to excuse my inattention by saying how hard it was to be a minister and how I was only trying to be a good provider. Now I know that I was investing my soul in my work, for it was there that I found my identity. Some memories are painful, indeed.

Now I am older and wiser. What really matters in life is not human achievement, but human connection. No one on his or her deathbed has ever said, "I wish I had spent more time at work." It is too late to turn back the clock and recover those lost years. But I refuse to torture myself with regrets over what might have been or with remorse over my failures. Older age brings a sense of perspective to see failures in the context of a whole life.

I find great joy in watching my sons as they take time for their children in ways that I never did. I am glad they learned the wisdom which I acquired only later in life. In *Sadhana* Anthony de Mello suggests a way to find healing of memories through prayer. "Return to some scene in the past where you have felt pain or grief or hurt or fear or bitterness. . . . Relive the event . . . But this time seek and find the presence of the Lord in it . . . In what way is he present there?"

"Whenever our hearts condemn us, God is greater than our hearts, and he knows everything" (1 John 3:20, AP). The healing of memories is found in the loving forgiveness and understanding of God.

EVER LOVING GOD:
You know our failures and you know our hearts.
Heal our painful memories of the past, that we may find joy
in the present.
AMEN.

35

Used-to-Beism
READ PSALM 31

I have passed out of mind like one who is dead;
I have become like a broken vessel.
(Psalm 31:12, RSV)

I HAD TO INTRODUCE MYSELF AT A MEETING as a retired person. It petrified me. Others there told where they worked or described their most recent trip or work-related project. My own description–"retired"–sounded so ominous, so empty. Two words seemed to fit, "has been." I managed to blurt out, "I am retired, but still active," as if I needed to apologize for no longer being in the full-time work force. I was a victim of the retirement disease known as "used-to-beism."

Saul, the first king of Israel, suffered from the same disease. At first his star had shone brightly. "There is none like him among all the people" (1 Samuel 10:24, RSV). He reached the pinnacle when he smashed the Ammonites, sent the Philistines scurrying back to their land, and vanquished Israel's enemies. But he could not win the inner battle and began to be threatened by the loss of his throne. David becomes his therapist, but also his rival. Soon, David, with his smashing victories and charismatic personality, eclipses Saul and Saul is rejected as king.

Saul's decline is vividly seen in scenes from the wilderness of Ziph, where David spares his life. "Behold, I have played the fool, and have erred exceedingly," he says (1 Samuel 26:21, RSV). Saul is a tragic hero, more to be understood than condemned, one who errs but whose story points the way to wholeness.

Nothing creates more depression in retirement years than the feeling of uselessness. Nothing hurts more than feeling you are "out of mind like one who is dead." No one likes to think of themselves as a person who *used-to-be* valued, productive, and of worth.

Life is not to be seen as a peak, with an upward and downward side, as if retirement means automatic consignment to the world of has-beens. Life has peaks and valleys at any age. And I cannot but believe that there is more for us to do in the midst of life beside simply watch it from the balcony.

Retirement is an opportunity, not a fate; an enrichment, not a diminishment. It is a beginning, no less challenging because it is the beginning of an end. I think of another Saul, who later became Paul. His life was crowned with service to the very end. His epitaph might have been, "I have fought the good fight, I have finished the race, I have kept the faith" (2 Timothy 4:7, RSV). To his final breath, he pressed on for the upward calling of God in Christ Jesus. That is the spirit every retired person needs when others look on him or her as a "used-to-be."

GOD OF THE MORNING, NOON, AND EVENING OF LIFE:
Help us to find new challenges and joys in our retired years
with the confidence that "He who began a good work in us
will bring it to completion at the day of Jesus Christ."
AMEN.

36

Rejection
READ MARK 12:1-12

Have you not read this scripture, "The very stone which the builders rejected has become the head of the corner, this was the Lord's doing, and it is marvelous in our eyes"?
(Mark 12:10-11, RSV)

SOONER OR LATER IN LIFE everyone will experience rejection. It may be that you were bypassed in the school play or the last to be chosen in pickup games at school. It may have been that you were turned down for a long-anticipated promotion or lost a position in the world of work. Such rejection makes one leery, cautious, and restrained.

Retired persons face rejection, too. It is the feeling that others discount us because we are no longer in the mainstream of life. Often when retired persons seek part-time employment and are not accepted, it adds further to the feeling of being unfit and unusable.

Sometimes we pretend that it doesn't really matter but it does. We say, "I couldn't care less," and what we really mean is "I wish I didn't care so much." Being discarded, feeling unwanted, being passed over for someone else is hard to take. Fear of rejection is particularly difficult for retired persons because it robs us of courage. So we withdraw into turtle time and surrender to self-pity. We cringe from new experiences.

Remember Jesus, who experienced rejection on this earth. "He was despised and rejected of men. . . ." From his first sermon in Nazareth's synagogue to his last act on Golgotha's cross, he was rejected. His own family, friends, and disciples turned away from him.

Yet he never surrendered to self-pity or despair. His life was grounded in God, so he could live without human approval. "The very stone which the builders rejected has become the head of the corner." He transformed rejections into resurrections.

G. Campbell Morgan, who became a prince of the pulpit, applied for the Wesleyan ministry in 1888, but he failed the preaching examination. Dejected, he wrote his father a letter that contained one word—"Rejected." The reply was quick. "Rejected on earth. Accepted in Heaven." Fear of rejection is rooted in our profound need to be loved, yet only God can love us completely.

It takes faith not to be defeated by rejection. It takes courage to rise above these feelings of being of no value, to turn our lives in new directions. We may be the stone which the builders reject; they may discard us as non-productive. But by faith we can discover new possibilities in the Third Age.

INEXHAUSTIBLE GOD:
When we are rejected, your approval and love energizes us to try again. Give us courage to find new possibilities, even when all doors seem to be shut.
AMEN.

37

Crumbs from the Table
READ MATTHEW 15:21-28

[Jesus] replied, "It is not right
to take the children's bread and toss it to their dogs."
"Yes, Lord," she said, "but even
the dogs eat the crumbs that fall from their master's table."
Jesus answered, "Woman, you have great faith."
(Matthew 15:26-28, NIV)

THE PERSISTENT FAITH OF THE CANAANITE WOMAN is
one of the Bible's great stories. When she first begs for
help for her daughter, Jesus seems to put her on hold.
His silence seems out of character to us. When rebuked
for asking for "bread" that belongs to Gentiles, she begs
for crumbs from their table. Jesus rewards her persistent
faith with healing for her daughter.

The story became alive for me while talking with an
older widow who still worked as a church secretary.
She said, "It's all well and good for people to plan retirement, but that's fantasy for me. I can't retire on my
social security check, and my aging parents are sick and
need my help. I'm stuck in this job for quite a while."

She points up one of the real retirement issues that
women face. On one hand, financial realities must be
faced. Today's twenty-five-year-old woman who retires
after working until sixty can expect the same retirement
benefits that her mother received (adjusted only for
inflation). Yet her mother may never have earned wages
or paid social security taxes. Despite more women in
the workplace, the percentage receiving a dependent's

benefit at retirement has remained constant at sixty-two per cent. For many women, the *golden* years become the *beholdin'* years. On the other hand, caregiving duties continue to fall primarily on women. Seven out of ten primary caregivers are women, who spend an average of sixteen hours a week caring for an aging parent.

Some men are becoming more involved in caring for aging parents, but most are not taking more time away from work to do so. Women average 11.5 years away from work; men average 1.3. Instead of more men remaining home for caregiving, women are assuming the roles of breadwinner *and* caregiver. Such responsibility causes women untold stress, whether they still work or are forced to stay home to care for aging parents.

As Americans grow older, the burden of caregiving increases. It is not uncommon for women in their seventies to be caring for aging parents in their nineties. And as society grows older, the question becomes: Who will care for the next generation of aging parents?

I saw a sign over the desk of a woman executive: WORK FOR THE LORD. THE PAY ISN'T GREAT, BUT THE RETIREMENT PLAN IS OUT OF THIS WORLD. I admit the truth of the sign, for our real treasures are in heaven, not on earth. But Jesus also said, "The worker deserves his (her) wages" (Luke 10:7). We must ease the burden for women who are both homemakers and wage-earners. Respite care, pension reform, and enlightened social security policies are part of the answer. Only then can the persistent cries of so many be answered.

PROTECTOR OF JUSTICE:
You always stand with the disadvantaged and unprotected.
We ask your help for those in their retirement years who
bear the heavy burden of caring for aging parents without
adequate resources. Convert our concern into action.
AMEN.

V

JOURNEY TO WHOLENESS

*Perhaps we should
stop using the word retirement
with all its negative connotations,
and use instead the concept of freedom.
Freedom to read, to interact socially and to learn;
freedom to change one's lifestyle
and set priorities based on contemplation
and absence of social pressures.*

MAXWELL JONES

38

The Healing Silence
READ MARK 1:35-39

*"For God alone my soul waits in silence;
from him comes my salvation."*
(Psalm 62:1, RSV)

TODAY I TORE MYSELF AWAY FROM PEOPLE and sought solitude in the mountains. I was two miles from the nearest person and had time for silent walks along the trails. It was strange at first but I learned to listen to the "sounds of silence" and became aware of the depths of an inner life that is available if we seek it. Along those peaceful mountain trails, amid the silence of eternity, I felt centered, at peace. The silence was incredible.

Ours is a noisy culture and even in retirement days we can succumb to "the fleeting fashions of the age" (Romans 12:2, MOFFATT). For most people silence creates nervousness and restlessness. Silence is even seen as a kind of deviant behavior. "She seems quiet," we say, as if it is some kind of strange behavior. Imposed silence often creates hostility and resentment. If silence is golden, then most of us are bankrupt.

And yet, in memory of a loss, we pause for a moment of silence. Or responding to some great moment, we tend to be silent. Peter described the Christian's experience as one of unspeakable joy. Is it not true that silence becomes the best tribute to a moment of unspeakable joy?

We all have our own mental pictures of Jesus: the compassionate lover of our souls, the playful friend of children, the loving advocate of outcasts. One that haunts me is the image of the praying Christ, the one who left the crowds and even his closest friends to be alone in the silence.

Donald X. Burt well says, "Now that I have come to age, I perceive a natural stillness forced upon me. I am now out of the mainstream. . . . I live now only in a quiet present. . . . My present moments are now more like warm lava slowly moving over the landscape, hiding the fire within. Stillness has been given to me."

`In these redirected days of retirement, I am learning how to be quiet. It has helped me renew a sense of at-oneness with myself. I know now how distracted and distressed I had been, like a rubber band stretched to its absolute limit. Life takes on new meaning now: the beauty of nature, the mystic quiet of a mountain stream, the flowers of spring. I am getting in touch with my life present and past, with the people in my midst and with those gone before.

Silence heals. It puts us in touch with God. As the psalmist wrote, "For God alone my soul waits in silence." Not in the discordant noise of our chatty culture, but in the incredible silence, God comes. And that Presence gives us strength to grapple with life. How poor we are without this silence!

SUSTAINER OF LIFE:
When will we learn that without your presence, we are poor, wretched, miserable, blind beings? Teach us to be still, and in the silence, may we find that life which is life indeed.
AMEN.

39

Striking Sails
READ ACTS 27:1-8

*As the wind did not allow us to go on,
we sailed under the lee of Crete off Salmone.
Coasting along with it with difficulty,
we came to a place called Fair Havens.
(Acts 27:7–8, RSV)*

PAUL WAS EMBARKED ON HIS LAST JOURNEY, the long awaited trip to Rome. At Myra, he and his friends found a ship from Alexandria bound for Rome. Strong west winds made the direct journey impossible so they came to a little port called Fair Havens. There, for a while, they had to strike sails and wait.

Striking sails is a powerful image of retirement life. The days of hoisting sails in youth, leaving the harbor for the open seas, are almost over. The time has come to strike sails in the safe harbor of the Third Age of life.

I realized now how very much I was controlled by the routine of a regimented life–going to the office, seeing the same people, going through motions. But several years ago I slowed down the pace, broke out of the grave clothes of conformity and began to develop other interests: listening to music, learning photography, walking. Now I know this was all preparation for the striking of the sails.

I remember what it felt like to be at the beach after the summer vacationers had left. There was something mystic about the hush that fell in those September days when the crowds were gone and there was a touch of autumn in the air. The slower pace of life often made me feel that the after season was the best time of all at the beach. So it is with retirement. I have learned to strike the sails, to rest, and to participate in life in a more distanced way, free from the pressure of performance. There is still much to do, but it is liberating to know I don't have to do it; I have time for priorities.

Paul made it to Rome and later wrote to Timothy, "For I am already on the point of being sacrificed; the time of my departure has come" (2 Timothy 4:6, RSV). This time he spoke of loosing a ship from its moorings so that it might get out of port into the open sea. The voyage, called death, was a departure into a larger life, a life that is free from all restraints.

For now, I enjoy the rest. It is good to sing and dance and rejoice and to celebrate the moments.

O LORD:
Support us all the day long,
until the shadows lengthen, and the evening comes,
and the busy world is hushed, and the fever of life is over,
and our work is done. Then in your mercy grant us a safe
lodging, and a holy rest, and peace at the last;
through Jesus Christ our Lord.
AMEN.
(Prayer by John Henry Newman 1801-1890)

40

Addicted to Books
READ 2 TIMOTHY 4:9-18

When you come,
bring the cloak that I left with Carpus at Troas,
also the books, and above all the parchments.
(2 Timothy 4:13, RSV)

YEARS OF READING PAUL'S LETTERS convinces me that invariably he added to them a postscript that contains gems of wisdom. While writing to Timothy, he adds one that tells us what Paul considered important late in life. He asks Timothy to bring his cloak, the books, and "above all the parchments" (the scriptures of the Old Testament, no doubt). Books were important to Paul.

I confess I am a bookaholic. I find myself in retirement spending endless hours in libraries just reading for pleasure. No longer bound by the need to do research or write sermons, I can play the serendipity game. That means moving slowly among the shelves of books, hoping for an unexpected discovery. There are times that a book finds me.

So much hype has been given to the importance of exercise in our later years to keep our bodies fit. You don't hear as much about the inner fitness that comes through reading great literature. The diet of the mind is important too, and the modern addiction to television is robbing our spirits.

Nothing concerns me as much in these days of extending our years of life than that we should become a nation of older people who do nothing but stare at television or chase our hobbies. "The life of the mind is the service of God."

Spiritual reading is a means of grace. In his *Confessions*, Augustine tells of hearing the voice of a child in the garden saying, Pick it up, read it; pick it up, read it." He took the book and read the words of Paul in Romans 13:13 and "there was infused in my heart something like the light of full certainty and all the gloom of doubt vanished away."

Says Quaker writer Elton Trueblood, reflecting on his life, "At home, there are books to be reread and other books to be read for the first time. Here they are in my library, waiting patiently for my attention; and now, at last, I have the time. I realize that we tend to read the great books too early, before we have enough experience to understand them."

In retirement years, we have a golden opportunity to become acquainted with the great spiritual classics. Rereading *The Great Devotional Classics,* a pamphlet series published by Upper Room Books has greatly enriched my soul.

Ministry and teaching, the two careers that claimed most of my professional life, demanded that I read a great deal. However, my reading in retirement is much different. Earlier I read for professional reasons, or to keep "intellectually respectable." Now my reading is for enjoyment, and spiritual nourishment.

Is it any wonder that Paul asked Timothy to bring the books to the prison in Rome? He knew their value. So, I'm a bookaholic, and that is a positive addiction.

ETERNAL SOURCE OF WISDOM:
Help us to realize that untapped resources of wisdom and beauty are found in books. Help us to turn from some of our preoccupations, that we may take time to read.
AMEN.

41

The Eleventh Hour Call
READ MATTHEW 20:1-16

And about the eleventh hour
he went out and found others standing idle, and said to them,
"Why have you been standing here idle all day?"
They said to him, "Because no one hired us."
He said to them, "You also go into the vineyard."
(Matthew 20:6-7 NKJV)

THE OWNER OF THE VINEYARD needed workers as late as the eleventh hour (five o'clock in the evening). It was harvest time and the rains were coming. So when he found these workers (older ones, perhaps, bypassed earlier by recruiters?), he asked why they stood idle in the village square. They replied, "Because no one hired us." He gave them work to do at the eleventh hour–for them and for him!

This is a parable for retirement. Some retired persons do not need to work, but many need to work part-time, and some even need to reenter the work force. We are just beginning to see the wisdom of hiring the retired. The problem is that many retired persons stand idle because no one will hire them.

Meaningful work is still a vital part of a creative retirement. I have found a compromise that has enabled me to enjoy retirement and yet keep a semblance of creative work. As an interim minister, I am no longer bound by the demands of full-time ministry. But the limited work I do gives me a sense of contributing something to the work for God's kingdom in the world. Even at the eleventh hour of my life.

The surprising story of the workers in the vineyard presents two ways of regarding our worth: grace and merit. The logic of merit views the world of work in everyday terms–we work and receive what we deserve. The logic of grace moves in a surprising way. It is all a gift of God.

Composer Lowell Mason wrote two hymns in his later years: "Nearer My God to Thee" (1862), and "Work, for the Night is Coming" (1874). In the latter hymn, Mason seems to imply that the night is held at bay by those who work. Night consists of non-working, non-creating, non-being. As long as we are involved in some creative work, then time is timeless, and we slow down the coming of the night. If we stay active and find some creative work, we will slow down the night when no one works.

Jesus said, "As long as it is day, we must do the work of him who sent me. Night is coming when no one can work" (John 9:4, NIV). Work for the kingdom never ends in this life. We are needed, just as the owner of the vineyard needed the workers at the eleventh hour. God comes to where you are standing in idleness or even despair, feeling that you are wasting your life, and says, "I want you."

The real question for retired persons is not "What did I retire from?" but rather "What did I return to?"

LORD OF LIFE:
We have retired from work,
but help us to realize that work for the kingdom never ends.
May we find our place in that work.
"Establish Thou the work of our hands, yea,
establish the work of our hands."
AMEN.

42

The Daily Discipline
READ 1 CORINTHIANS 9:24-27

*But I discipline my body,
and bring it unto subjection, lest, when I have preached to
others, I myself should become disqualified.
(1 Corinthians 9:27, NKJV)*

ONE OF THE DISCOVERIES I have made is the importance of walking every day. Everyone knows that walking helps our bodies and minds. The ancient writer of Ecclesiasticus said it well,

> Better a poor man healthy and fit
> Than a rich man tormented in his body.
> Health and strength are better than any gold
> A robust body than untold wealth.
> No riches can outweigh bodily health.
> –Ecclesiasticus 30:14-16, JB

But I am learning that walking is also good for the soul. For one thing, I can pray as I walk. And walking is a way to reflect, to draw back from the din and clatter, to behold the beauty of God's world.

When Paul wrote about the disciplined life, he used a metaphor drawn from the sporting arena. Paul's readers no doubt thought of the Isthmian Games, held every second year in a Corinthian suburb. Drawing from the games of boxing and running, Paul urges the Corinthians to run so as to obtain the prize of new life with God. He reminds his readers that "Everyone who competes in the games goes into strict training" (1

Corinthians 9:25, NIV). As athletes train, so Christians must submit to strict discipline and training if they want to be victorious in the struggle of life.

It is important that we make walking a daily discipline. Walking energizes us, clears our minds, and helps us to see beauty in nature. Joseph A. Sittler says, "When we go on wheels, we miss what can be seen only on foot. I am always mentioning to various friends who are sedentary and auto-trapped riders the things I see walking in my Chicago neighborhood–things they never see because they whiz past them in a car. . . . We rush through life and see the panoramic, but miss the microscopic."

There is something symbolic about taking a daily walk. We can rise to major crises and handle short-term emergencies. But so often we fail in the day-after-week-after-month walking that life requires. The ancient prophet said it well, "But those who hope in Yahweh renew their strength, they put out wings like eagles. They run and do not grow weary, walk and never tire" (Isaiah 40:31, JB). Being able to handle the day-by-day issues that older age brings is what it is all about.

In her book *Prayer and Our Bodies*, Flora Wuellner urges us to take "parable walks" in which we set out with no agenda but to ask God to show us something meaningful. She says, "There will be something God wants you to encounter . . . a memory, whose healing time has come, guidance for an unsolved problem, inner nurture, or a new insight." My daily discipline of walking has often brought such unexpected revelations.

INEXHAUSTIBLE GOD:
What resources of strength and vigor can be found in you
to renew our strength–but we must discipline ourselves.
Help us to get off the couch and get on the move.
AMEN.

43

The Book I Came Back To
READ LUKE 24:13-35

Oh, how I love your law!
I meditate on it all day long.
(Psalm 119:97, NIV)

THE ACCESS TO MORE TIME in my retirement has
provided me with opportunity to spend more time with
the Bible. The rich rewards of Bible study in recent
times have given us an increasing number of modern
translations that have added to our understanding of
the great Book. I have grown to appreciate the value of
quiet, reflective meditation on this living word.

Those two people on the road to Emmaus (possibly
Cleophas and his wife) had read the scriptures. But then
a Stranger walked the road with them and the
scriptures came alive with power and meaning. "Were
not our hearts burning within us while he talked with
us on the road and opened the Scriptures to us?" (Luke
24:32, NIV).

In later life I have learned the value of devotional
reading of the Bible. We do have this treasure in earthen
vessels. Critical study of the Bible can help to bring
meaning to the ancient texts, but we must beware of the
danger of replacing the Bible with books about the
Bible. In *Grace Abounding*, John Bunyan tells how he
read the Bible with new eyes. "Indeed, I was then never
out of the Bible." We need to shelve some books about
the Bible and turn to the book itself with new eyes. My
goal is that of the blessed man in Psalm 1, "his delight is

in the law of the LORD, and on his law he meditates day and night" (Psalm 1:2, NIV).

I have spent a lifetime listening to opinions about the Bible. All too often what we think the Bible means becomes more important than what it does say. I recall my impatience with my father years ago when he said that he did not read many theories about the Bible but rather spent his time reading its pages. I thought that somewhat naive but now I realize the wisdom of his words. Thomas à Kempis, the fourteenth century mystic wrote, "If the eternal Word speaks to a man he is delivered from many conjectures." In these redirected years, nothing is more important to me than listening with an open soul for God's word in scripture.

I discovered a role model in a nursing home, a ninety-four-year-old woman reading her Bible. She told me that her eyesight was growing dimmer every day, but "I save whatever eyesight I have left for reading the Bible. It is God's food for my soul." Her old eyes had found new light at the closing of day.

As Sir Walter Scott lay dying, he asked his attendant Lockhart to read to him. Seeing that there were thousands of volumes in the famous author's library, Lockhart asked from which book he should read. "Need you ask?" said Scott. "There is but one." Lockhart chose the fourteenth chapter of John's Gospel. "Well, this is great comfort," Scott observed. "I have followed you distinctly, and I feel as if I were to be myself again." The treasure is always available.

HIDDEN GOD:
You are present in scripture
if we will wait in silence for this treasure.
May we move beyond words on a page
to a living word inside our hearts.
AMEN.

44

Overcoming the Chicken Little Complex
READ MATTHEW 10:5-15

If anyone will not welcome you or listen to your words, shake the dust off your feet when you leave that home or town.
(Matthew 10:14, NIV)

CHICKEN LITTLE TOOK A STROLL through the woods one day. Her path took her under the limbs of an oak tree. As she walked underneath the tree, an acorn came loose and hit Chicken Little on the head. She did not see the acorn lying at her feet, only the sky above. She ran to tell the other animals in the barnyard "The sky is falling. The sky is falling!" It is true of us sometimes as well. Some little nuts hit our heads in life and we panic and think our world is coming to an end.

Jesus gave sound counsel to the first disciples when he told them not to panic if they were not received hospitably at every home or town on their missionary travels. "Shake the dust off your feet," and move on. Life is too short and too precious to let frustrations and rejections punish us.

In earlier days I was a victim of pyramid thinking (piling one imaginary thought on another), until the teetering stack of problems overwhelmed me. Some call it catastrophizing. As I let little acorns create near panic, my theme song was "Ain't It Awful." Now, I am learning to take things in stride and not expend endless energy in anxiety. Being delivered from others' expectations and my perfectionistic work style has given me a sense of peace.

Inner freedom always when we acknowledge the limitations of life. It was the apostle Paul who penned the words from prison, "I have learned, in whatever state I am, to be content" (Philippians 4:11, RSV). This did not mean that he was becoming complacent or unconcerned about further ministry. Even in Rome, he yearned to preach the gospel in Spain.

What Paul meant was that he could be independent of circumstances, that nothing could shake his inner peace. Joshua Loth Liebman said that when he was a brash youth, he compiled an inventory of things he desired from life: health, love, beauty, fame, fortune. He showed the list to a wise elder, and the old man said, "You have missed the most important thing. Without it, every possession becomes a torment." "What's that?" asked Liebman. The old man took a pencil and wrote, "Peace of mind."

Jesus said, "I came that they may have life, and have it abundantly" (John 10:10, RSV). Wholeness means our inner peace is not shaken by the events of life. In *Revelations of Divine Love*, Julian of Norwich writes: "He did not say, 'You shall not be tempest-tossed, you shall not be work-weary, you shall not be discomforted.' But he said, 'You shall not be overcome.'"

Troubles, distresses, and anxieties cannot be side-stepped in the retirement years. But realizing that God's grace can be counted upon to deliver us through these trials is assurance enough.

SOURCE OF PEACE:
Help us to find that perfect peace when our minds are stayed on you. May your peace, which passes all understanding, keep our hearts and minds in Christ Jesus.
AMEN.

45

It Is Also Blessed To Receive
READ JOHN 1:1-16

From his fulness have we all received, grace upon grace.
(John 1:16, RSV)

What have you that you did not receive?
(1 Corinthians 4:7, RSV)

A FRIEND OF MINE CHIDED ME RECENTLY about being a pensioner and not working full-time. He said, "Don't you feel guilty relying on your pension and the government instead of working full-time?" After joking that he was trying to lay a guilt trip on me, I began to process his question.

Paul Tournier distinguishes between "functional guilt" that results from social suggestion, and "value guilt" that is free judgment of the self by the self. I am sure that there are some in this workaholic society who believe that people that retire early are scroungers, living on the backs of those who are working. But, I earned my retirement, and it is also a touch of grace. No, I thought, I feel no guilt about early retirement.

The author of the fourth Gospel says, "Of his fulness have we all received, grace upon grace" (John 1:16, RSV), like the continual roll of waves upon the beach. Why is it that we allow our religion to be so work-oriented that we cannot experience grace? It seems that we have to be tough cowboys at the OK Corral, not taking anything from anyone. "Don't need any help, don't want any help, won't take any help," is the way some express it.

Some of our religion has taught us to give to others, help others, and care for others, but it has said little about us receiving from others or having our needs met by others. Sometimes we get the feeling that it is all right to "love our neighbors, but not our neighbors as ourselves." I know Jesus said, "It is more blessed to give than to receive" (Acts 20:35, RSV). But there are times when it is also blessed to receive! We need to receive as well as give, to be needy and care for ourselves as well as being caregivers.

Jesus himself knew how to receive. He received with grace the precious ointment from the woman, shortly before his cross and resurrection. He received it and celebrated it.

Retirement has re-taught me the primacy of grace, of receiving gifts which I may not deserve. It is good not to always be in control, to be so self-sufficient. I am receiving many gifts, not just senior discounts and financial gains. Friends have been gracious, people whom I served now minister to me. I have always believed that it is easier to give than to receive. But, I am learning to receive. Isn't that at least some of what Christianity is all about? "Nothing in my hand I bring, simply to Thy cross I cling." Perhaps we harm ourselves at times because our hands are so full with our work that we cannot receive the gift God gives us freely.

GRACIOUS AND GIVING GOD:
Teach us to receive as well as give.
Let our religion not be only caring for others,
but may it offer us opportunities to receive the gifts
that you send to us.
AMEN.

46

Victory over Ego
READ GALATIANS 2:17-22

I have been crucified with Christ
and I no longer live, but Christ lives in me.
The life I live in the body, I live by faith in the Son of God,
who loved me and gave himself for me.
I do not set aside the grace of God.
(Galatians 2:20–21, NIV)

ONE OF THE ACID TESTS OF THE CHRISTIAN LIFE is whether we practice this command of Christ: "If any want to become my followers, let them deny themselves and take up their cross and follow me" (Matthew 16:24, NRSV). It is not a matter of performance or observance but whether or not the spirit of Christ lives in us.

It is difficult to deny the ego, the self-centeredness within us that makes us measure all of life by its effect on our plans, hopes, and profit. Albert Edward Day said, "If you want to measure the selfish ego's tyranny over your consciousness, try to think of God for five minutes and see if even for that brief period you can keep *I*, *me*, and *mine* out of your thoughts."

Paul can claim that his ego had been crucified with Christ, so that now it is Christ who lives in him. The controls of his life had been surrendered to Christ and he had become a new creation. He had the kind of life only Jesus Christ could explain.

Retirement deals a blow to the ego. You are no longer in demand and your advice is no longer sought in power situations. At times you are forced into idleness and no longer get ego strokes from making things happen. The many ego gratifications from colleagues at work are gone, and without positive self-esteem, there can be a real void.

In a small way, retirement can be a paradigm of the Christian life–fewer ego strokes, removal from places of power, fewer opportunities for service. An early Christian hymn says that Christ "made Himself of no reputation, taking the form of a servant" (Philippians 2:7, NKJV). No reputation, no power, ego denied.

Christ marched to the sound of another drummer. While the disciples quarreled about preeminence and power, Jesus took a towel and basin of water, and washed their feet, a dirty job nobody wanted to do. His final reward was a cross, the ultimate proof of his love.

Jesus' words show the way: "Unless a grain of wheat falls into the ground and dies, it remains alone; but if it dies, it produces much grain. He who loves his life will lose it, and he who hates his life in this world will keep it for eternal life" (John 12:24–25, NKJV).

Christians who retire should take heart when they feel left out of power or deprived of the ego gratification from the world of work. It is a rare opportunity to follow Christ and to answer his call to service. Then *God* will exalt us and our satisfaction will come from doing God's work, not from the praise of others.

SERVANT GOD:
Give us the joy that comes through
denying our selfish ways and doing your work on earth.
Let us, with no thought for ourselves,
take up our cross and follow you.
AMEN.

47

Blessed!

READ GENESIS 27

And [Esau] said,
"Have you not reserved a blessing for me?"
(Genesis 27:36, NKJV)

THE COVER OF *THE NEW YORKER* magazine showed a cartoon depicting an elderly gentleman standing in his pajamas and robe at his apartment door. He has just secured the door for the night with not one, but four locks. Only after the last lock was fastened did he notice a small white envelope stuck under the door. On the envelope was a large heart-shaped sticker. His private security system had been broken through. Someone got in—with a valentine! Love had found a way.

Retired people need to be blessed. Sometimes we feel like Esau did when Jacob stole his blessing from Isaac. Esau turns to his blind father and cries, "Have you not reserved a blessing for me?" We need to be loved and affirmed in this time of our lives when so much has been taken from us.

I know that we are to love others and meet their needs, but in retirement we have a special need to be loved and affirmed. Too often in our past we have looked for the blessing in our work and in our compulsive need to succeed. Some of us even reasoned, "If my parents can't bless me, maybe my work can." But the blessing doesn't come from impersonal sources, in response to our achievements. It comes from persons, in response to our soul.

Spiritual friendships bless us. The relationship between David and Jonathan was such a friendship. "And it was so . . . that the soul of Jonathan was knit to the soul of David, and Jonathan loved him as his own soul" (1 Samuel 18:1, NKJV). We need a soul-friend, one who walks the same journey as we do, with whom we can be at one, and through whom we can find atonement with all. Finding this friend is a blessing.

Family and others can bless us as well. Instead of living in a self-imposed isolation, where we can never be blessed, we must reach out to others. One retired woman who volunteered for work in a nursing home told me that, "Those frail older people have blessed me more than I could ever bless them. Their appreciation and acceptance brought new meaning to my life."

I experienced this in a powerful way recently when we cared for two of our grandchildren. My four-year-old grandson Daniel and I had spent some time sailing boats in a creek in back of our house. Suddenly, with no prompting from me, Daniel exclaims, "I love you Grandpa." I was blessed!

Ultimately, all blessing comes from God. We don't generate it, we participate in it. Jacob learned that lesson, when at Peniel he cried out in the midnight struggle, "I will not let you go, unless you bless me" (Genesis 32:26, RSV). God's blessing is often mediated through other people and comes to rest on us. The journey to wholeness in the retirement years is made easier when we experience this blessedness.

O LORD:
We are humbled by the power of someone's blessing.
As we give thanks, we ask for generous hearts
to be able to receive and pass on to another
the blessing that comes from you.
AMEN.

48

Music Came Back into My Life

READ PSALM 96

For lo, the winter is past, the rain is over and gone.
The flowers appear on the earth, the time of singing has come.
(Song of Solomon 2:11–12, RSV)

ALL MY LIFE I HAVE BEEN A LOVER OF MUSIC. It has been one way that I have found solitude and peace. The great classical music of the centuries and the hymns of the church have rescued me from despair and guided me through deep waters more often than I can recount. Martin Luther wrote, "Music is the greatest gift, indeed it is divine; and therefore Satan is extremely hostile to it, because by its influence many great temptations are overcome. The devil doesn't stay where there is music."

Although music has always blessed my life, I confess that in the last years of my active ministry, I found myself spending too much time too preoccupied with my work. The result was that music went out of my life.

Now, with more time for the life of the soul, music has come back in to my life. I have always been a lover of the classics, but now I am taking time to really listen to the immortal works of Bach, Beethoven, Mozart, and others. Music resounds in my study every day and it has become a gift of grace for these retirement days.

There is a parenthesis of music around all the great events of holy history. Job speaks of the day of creation "when the morning stars sang together, and all the heavenly beings shouted for joy" (Job 38:7, NRSV). All nature sang for God. When Yahweh delivered Israel from bondage, Moses celebrated the victory at the Red Sea with a song, "I will sing to the Lord, for he has triumphed gloriously; the horse and his rider he has thrown into the sea" (Exodus 15:1, RSV). The Psalms are the music of Israel that reflect our moods as well. As an early church father said, "The rest of the Bible speaks to you; the Psalms speak for you."

Music is also at the heart of the Christian faith. The birthnight of the Lord is celebrated by the singing of angels. Jesus sang the Hallel Psalms on the night of his betrayal. And no description of the Christian life is more poignant than that of Paul and Silas singing hymns at midnight in a Philippian jail (Acts 16:25). The Book of Revelation resounds with the choirs of God singing hymns of praise to the Lamb.

So, music has come back into my life. It has always been there in a way, but now I can hear it again. I believe that there is something symbolic in its return. Retirement has given me opportunity to be restored in soul, to be freed from the burdens of life, to sing and rejoice and dance once more.

O sing to the Lord a new song,
For he has done marvelous things!
–*Psalm 98*

CREATOR OF GOODNESS AND BEAUTY:
We thank you for the music you send into our lives.
May its joy and light restore our souls.
AMEN.

VI

Finding
that Creative Balance

*The man
who retired at the turn of the century
had a life expectancy of two years. His plans quite
appropriately included rest and leisure.
The man or woman of today
who anticipates 20 years of good health
would do well to design a new beginning.
Twenty years is too long to sit on any shelf,
no matter how comfortable.*

Louise McCants *and*
Cavette Robert

49

Pursuing that Second Career
READ NUMBERS 8:15-26

*At the age of fifty, they must retire from their regular service
and work no longer. They may assist their brothers in
performing their duties at the Tent of Meeting,
but they themselves must not do the work.*
(Numbers 8:25–26, NIV)

WHEN THEY REACHED THE AGE OF FIFTY, the Levites
were released from routine work, no longer taking their
place in the regular work of the community, free from
the more exacting duties that would tax their physical
strength. They could pursue a second career, which for
them was voluntary ministry in the holy place, teaching
the law, or other more distinctive spiritual functions.

Paul Tournier believes retired persons need a second
career that must be distinguished from leisure activity.
He insists that second careers have goals and a mission,
with precedence over more selfish pleasures. He says
that such careers "will have no age-limit, no routine, no
fixed wage tied to an obligation to work. It can be
voluntary, it can be paid, but without any compulsory
relationship between earnings and output. It has
nothing to do, therefore, with the idea of a second *job*."

Last week I talked with a retired man who said that
his wife had died some months ago, but despite his
grief, he said he didn't have time to fret. He was a
volunteer driver for a social center, transporting frail
elderly to doctors' offices, social services, and shopping
areas. For him, it was a new career.

Anticipating my retirement some years ago, I developed a vital interest in aging. I spent valuable time developing new programs and services for older persons in our community. Now that concern has become a second career. I have learned that people who enjoy retirement the most are those who created commitments and interests outside their jobs long before they stopped working. It seems we must retire *before* we retire, and we must develop attachments and involvements outside our jobs. Now that I am retired, I have ample time to devote to my second career, working with frail elderly in the community, doing life review groups in nursing homes, and helping older church members remember and record their faith stories.

It is said that one day Michelangelo entered his studio to examine the work of his students. As he came to the painting of one of his favorite students, he stood and looked at it for a long time. Then, to the utter surprise of the class, he suddenly took a brush and wrote one word across the canvas–*amplius,* meaning larger. He was not rejecting the student's work but the small size of the canvas had made its design look cramped. It needed to be expanded.

In our retirement years, we may find that God calls us to second careers where the word *amplius* is written across our work. We can expand our horizons, widen our outreach, and discover new careers in this freer, yet more challenging Third Age of life.

INEXHAUSTIBLE GOD:
We are called to create second careers in our retirement years.
Help us to be responsive to your call and
find new fulfillment in our chosen second careers.
AMEN.

50

Don't Write My Epitaph Yet

READ PHILIPPIANS 3:7-16

Brethren, I do not consider that I have made it my own;
but one thing I do, forgetting what lies behind and straining
forward to what lies ahead, I press on toward the goal
for the prize of the upward call of God in Christ Jesus.
(Philippians 3:13–14, RSV)

I have been busy collecting epitaphs about people who retire.

> Old teachers never die; they just lose their principals.
> Old lawyers never die; they just lose their appeal.
> Old doctors never die; they just lose their patience.
> Old framers never die; they just hang it up.
> Old preachers never die; they just go on and on.

What bothers me about these sayings is that they make retirement a time of passivity and inertia. They are ageist statements and they bypass the creative possibilities for meaningful activity that retirement affords.

Near the end of his life, while imprisoned in Rome, Paul wrote to the Philippians that he was still pressing on for the prize. He has not yet realized the prize. Past achievements were forgotten. The word he uses for "straining forward" is the same word about a racer going hard for the finish line. It describes him with eyes for nothing but the goal. To the very end the Christian life is the life of an athlete pressing onward to a goal which is always out in front. We are called to forget past achievements, and press on for the high calling of God in Christ Jesus.

As Christians, we are called at retirement to continue our race for the goal of Christian maturity as long as we live. The anonymous epitaph found in England for a blacksmith is not applicable.

> My goals are spent
> My iron's gone
> My nails are drove
> My work is done

We may have retired from full time work, but there is no retirement from the Christian life of creativity, caring, and work. It is senseless to dump men and women of surpassing skills and continuing creativity into the concentration camp of "old age" simply because we retire.

I have come to realize that spirituality is much more than silence, solitude, contemplation, and centeredness. Spirituality is also an active life of creativity and caring. Driven more by inner choice than outer demand, creativity gives opportunity to give birth to something new in our later years; caring is compassion reaching out to others. Paul exemplified this spirit in his later years. The end of life was not a time for inactivity or boredom but for new bursts of energy, new creations, and new caring for others.

Don't write epitaphs for us retired people just yet.

GOD OF THE BEGINNING, GOD OF THE END:
Deliver us from thinking that retirement is the end.
Lift our vision to see it as a new beginning.
AMEN.

51

Learning Detachment
READ MATTHEW 6:19-23

The eye is the lamp of the body. If your eyes are good, your whole body will be full of light. But if your eyes are bad, your whole body will be full of darkness.
(Matthew 6:22–23, NIV)

I HAVE ALWAYS LIKED THE STORY of two Zen monks returning to their monastery that lay some miles back from the bank of a river they had to cross. When they reached the ford, they saw a beautiful woman who feared to make the crossing. The elder monk, seeing her plight, put her on his shoulders and carried her to the opposite bank. After he set her down, they continued on their journey. They walked in silence for awhile, after which the younger man exclaimed, "Whatever made you carry that woman across the river?" "Good gracious," came the reply, "are you still carrying her?"

In our retirement years, we need to learn detachment, to learn not to carry our past anxieties and burdens. Although we are liberated from some compulsions and anxieties from the world of work, we may still allow ourselves to be bogged down with attachments.

Detachment is like getting a clear signal on the television. It means being free from being victimized by our own emotions and problems. Jesus knew the value of having single-mindedness of soul. "If your eyes are good your whole body will be full of light."

Being detached means that we can enter into relationships with other people without contaminating them with our problems. Detachment means we know ourselves so well that we have a perspective upon our reactions to other people. Being detached means we are freer to discover a committed relationship to God. According to Meister Eckhart, detachment "enkindles the heart, awakens the spirit, stimulates our longings, and shows us where God is." No wonder Jesus said, "Blessed are the pure in heart, for they shall see God" (Matthew 5:8, RSV).

In conversation with a friend who had retired, and then returned to a full-time position, I shared my newfound joy in finding detachment. It was so easy to become attached to the demands and pressures of full-time work. Now, I am free to experience God's presence in the midst of life. Is it any wonder that his hymn "Dear Lord and Father of Mankind" John Greenleaf Whittier contained those immortal words about solitude written when he was sixty-five?

> Drop Thy still dews of quietness,
> Till all our strivings cease;
> Take from our souls the strain and stress,
> And let our ordered lives confess
> The beauty of Thy peace.

He knew what it was to live in grace, to have singleness of eye, to be detached. It is possible for anyone, especially for those who now have fewer demands after retirement.

KEEPER OF OUR SOULS:
You guard us all throughout life, and preserve our going out and our coming in. Help us to find the centeredness, the single-mindedness which alone gives peace.
AMEN.

52

Hanging in the Balance
READ ECCLESIASTES 7:13-22

The [one] who fears God will avoid all extremes.
(Ecclesiastes 7:18, NIV)

I VISITED AN OLD CLASSMATE TODAY who really had retired. He told me, "Three years ago I retired and I was so tired that all I wanted to do was rest. So I piddle around at home, sleep late, read the papers, and forget the rest." I wonder how much longer he will continue in this laid-back lifestyle.

When I retired, some of my friends offered me this advice: "Just take it easy. You've earned a long rest." I admit it was refreshing at first. There is a time to do nothing. But after a few months, it got old. T.S. Eliot comments on the boredom of our modern wasteland, and shows us in J. Alfred Prufrock a man whose days had no meaning.

> For I have known them all already, known them all—
> Have known the evenings, mornings, afternoons,
> I have measured out my life with coffee spoons.

I have found that the best lifestyle for me is one of balance between vital involvement and creative solitude. The wise householder seeks the balance between things old and new. My quest is to find that delicate balance between rest and involvement.

I have learned how to rest. In a real sense, that has come about by way of a rediscovery of the Christian gospel that we are justified by faith and our acceptance does not depend on what we do, but on God's grace. Now that I'm less involved with work, I have found time to be available, first to myself, then to my family, and then to the world.

But I still like vital involvement in projects of my choosing. Working with small churches, helping at the soup kitchen, and listening to the faith stories of older people have helped me maintain my spiritual life. As Helen Hayes said, "Life begins at retirement–not because your job is finally behind you but because the world is suddenly opening up before you, and you've prepared yourself for your debut."

In the months since retirement, I have lived through many stages. The honeymoon felt good but it didn't last. I learned the sad lesson of becoming distracted by busyness until depression set in. Now I have attained some stability by this new life which seeks creative balance between rest and work.

I begin to get a glimpse now that retirement is an invitation that God is extending to us–a grace that allows us to move from the many things to one necessary thing. God comes to people in different ways during their lives, but at retirement God comes in a special way. For me that way is finding the creative balance.

GOD OF ALL GENERATIONS:
We pray that our lives may reflect that creative balance
between meaningful work and spiritual renewal.
AMEN.

53

Rewriting the Retirement Script
READ 1 THESSALONIANS 4:9-12

*But we exhort you . . . to do so more and more,
to aspire to live quietly, to mind your own affairs,
and to work with your hands.
(1 Thessalonians 4:10–11, RSV)*

JUST AS SURELY AS ANY SCRIPT ON PAPER defines the movements and speech of the players in a play, so there is a retirement script that far too many people live out. That script calls for withdrawal from life.

In Laurel Creek, West Virginia, sociologists John Lozier and Ronald Althouse discovered a cultural phenomenon in that rural Appalachian town called "retirement to the porch." The porch is a place of honor where social interactions occur and valued citizens receive visitors or have others pick up their groceries or do other errands. To retire to the porch, a person needs to have a good amount of social standing.

Although this may be a good practice for that small town, "retirement to the porch" can have negative meaning for many retired persons. It can mean being removed from the center of life, no longer in the mainstream of activities, "out to pasture," if you will.

The Christians at Thessalonica had "retired to the porch" because they believed the second coming of Jesus was imminent. They had given up their daily work and were upsetting everyone with their talk of Jesus' coming. Paul urged them not to retire but to be active, for the best way to commend Christianity to the outsider was by the daily diligence of their lives. Quiet and useful work is what is needed for the kingdom.

One of the retirement signs I see most often reads:

RETIRED
No Clock, No Phone
No Address, No Money

It seems to perpetuate the retirement script that retirement means inactivity and uselessness. In light of my experience and that of countless other vital, involved retirees, we need to alter that sign, so that it reads like this:

REDIRECTED
No Compulsions, No Pretense
No Laziness, No Hurry

Many people retire *from* something–a demanding job, a feeling of burnout, complex work assignments. But many do not know what they are retiring *to*. Retirement is a time for redirection, creative involvement and new beginnings but it is also a time for harvesting what we have sown. This is the new script the must replace the old script calling for retirement to the porch.

GOD OF HOPE AND JOY:
Let us see the hope
for new directions in our retirement years.
Let us find the joy that can only come
through vital involvement.
AMEN.

54

For Better, for Worse, and for Lunch

READ ACTS 18:1-3

Greet Prisca and Aquila, my fellow workers in Christ Jesus, who risked their necks for my life, to whom not only I but also all the churches of the Gentiles give thanks.
(Romans 16:3–4, RSV)

ONE OF THE SUBTLE DANGERS in retirement years is its possible effect on a marriage. At retirement, husbands and wives come face to face unlike any other time in their lives.

If the wife has fulfilled most of the homemaker functions, her private world is now being invaded and this can cause tensions. The old joke–"I married him for better, for worse, but not for lunch"– rings true for some couples. One frazzled woman told me, "I'm going crazy with Jack underfoot all the time. He is tired of playing golf all the time. I never knew retirement could be so disruptive."

On the other hand, husbands often fear the "honey-do" syndrome–the fear that their wives will control their free hours after retirement with a multitude of little jobs.

Prisca and Aquila were a remarkable older couple who formed a friendship with Paul at Corinth. Prisca, whose name meant "little old woman" is mentioned first in three of the six references to the couple. As it was unusual in those times for a wife to be mentioned before her husband, we may assume she was the stronger personality. Whenever they are mentioned in Paul's letters, there is a church in their home. Friendship, fellowship, and love seem to have radiated from their home.

In the example of Prisca and Aquila, we find a couple who are partners in the joint enterprise of the gospel. Their closeness provides a good model for retirement couples. The final reference to Prisca and Aquila is found in the second letter to Timothy (4:9). "Greet Prisca and Aquila." Late in life, this couple is still active in the life of the church. In the early church they stand out as two bright and shining jewels in the crown of faith.

What we have discovered in retirement years is that a couple brings to these years the marriage they have created. If a couple has developed intimacy and closeness before retirement, there will be little difference in these redirected years. The bonds of intimacy and love present in pre-retirement years will only grow deeper in retirement.

Retirement years brings precious opportunities for couples to redirect. Freed from pressures at work and from supporting families, new directions can be taken–sharing mutual interests, new travels, time with grandchildren. Retirement couples may not ride into the sunset singing "Happy Trails," but they can redeem the time with new joys. Retired couples may well find that their marriage is reinvented and renewed.

MAKER OF MAN AND WOMAN:
If we are so fortunate to be a couple in these retirement years, help us to grow together in new directions. May our love for each other reflect your abiding love for us.
AMEN.

55

A Declaration of Interdependence
READ 1 CORINTHIANS 12:4-27

For as the body is one and has many members, but all the members of that one body, being many, are one body so also is Christ. For by one Spirit we were all baptized into one body.
(1 Corinthians 12:12–13, NKJV)

PEOPLE WHO RETIRE ARE FACED WITH endless challenges in interpersonal relationships, most of them different from earlier days. The loss of friends from work is real; one soon finds that the common bond that sustained those friendships has gone. Other relationships must be found to replace the daily camaraderie at work.

The family network also changes. Husbands and wives must coexist daily in the same space and face reinventing their relationship. Too often, adult children unload their problems on retired parents and instead of receiving support, parents are still having to provide it. It is difficult to build new friendships when confronted with lingering "adult children" problems. Moving away to new locations also shrinks the circle of friends.

The need for a new social network for retired persons is crucial. In their significant book, *Transitions: A Woman's Guide to Successful Retirement,* therapists Diana Cort-Van Arsdale and Phyllis Newman maintain that "many retired women felt that the need for friendship during the early years of their retirement was more intense than at any time since adolescence." The same is true for retired men, who often retreat into a self-imposed isolation with few social contacts.

What retired persons need to learn is the value of interdependence. We do not want to be "lone rangers," but we are terrified at the thought of increased dependence on others, especially family members. We need to rediscover Paul's concept of interdependence that he described in the Corinthian letter.

This interdependence is a unity in diversity, a bond that unites people. One can be free and maintain one's identity, and yet not be cut off from community. Paul speaks of a diversity of gifts, but all of them are used to build up the body of Christ. Each contributes to the whole and the whole depends on the healthy functioning of each member. Although we usually think of the church as we read these words, it is also true of generations in the body of Christ. We need each other. There can be no such thing as isolation in the church for young or old.

One of the alarming results of retirement communities is a kind of geriatric segregation. The church needs to define ways to create communities of faith where its older and younger members depend on each other.

Ben Jonson wisely said, "True happiness consists not in the multitude of friends, but in the worth and choice." Confronted with the loss of friends from work and the increasing demands of family, retired persons need well-chosen, dependable friends.

FRIEND AND CREATOR:
You are our one true friend,
and we praise you for your constant love and support.
Help us to find human friends in these days upon whom
we can depend and who will depend on us.
AMEN.

56

Investing in Someone's Future
READ JEREMIAH 32:1-15

Cast your bread on the water;
at long last you will find it again.
(Ecclesiastes 11:1, JB)

Do not forget: thin sowing means thin reaping;
the more you sow, the more you reap."
(2 Corinthians 9:6, JB)

JEREMIAH DID A STRANGE THING. His beloved land was being overrun by a foreign dictator who was inching ever closer every day to the capture of Jerusalem. The prophet himself was under house arrest by his own people for his "traitorous" counsel to surrender to this invader. His hometown of Anathoth was already in enemy hands. Yet, in that bleak moment, Jeremiah purchased a plot of ground at Anathoth. He had no guarantee that either he or any of his family would ever live on that land.

Jeremiah believed in the future, that God's word would be fulfilled, that "houses and fields and vineyards shall again be bought in this land" (Jeremiah 32:15, RSV). In a moment when all life seemed so hopeless, desperate, and final, he took a risk of faith. Faith is not belief in spite of evidence; it is life in scorn of consequence.

Jeremiah fully realized that the purchase of Anathoth real estate was not for his own sake. He knew he would never live on that land, nor would any of his family for a long time. The exile into Babylon was ahead and Jeremiah knew that. But his simple act of buying that real estate was an investment in the future.

I keep an ancient saying on my study wall that I often think about these days. "The beginning of wisdom comes when a person plants trees, the shade under which they know they will never sit." Erikson calls it *generativity*, the concern for establishing and guiding the next generation. So these are the days when we need to invest in the future, to help the children and grandchildren find their way.

The word of God to Jeremiah was not, "Guard what you have, Jeremiah. Never mind what's happening outside in the street, or why be anxious about the future. Look out for yourself." Rather, God's word was, "Buy a field. Invest in the future. Remember the next generation."

I saw a living example of this spirit while visiting a childcare center recently. I saw a retired teacher sitting in the midst of the children, captivating them with her humor and stories. She had retired from teaching and yet continued to invest her life in the future generations. Indeed, she had cast her bread upon the waters and her influence continued.

We can become so self-centered and narcissistic in these days of retirement. God's call is to invest in someone's future, to be someone's tomorrow.

GIVER OF LOVE:
Fill us with love for future generations,
and help us to find some way, however small,
to invest our lives for their sake.
AMEN.

57

Gifts from Grandchildren
READ MATTHEW 18:1-5

And calling to him a child, he put him in the midst of them,
and said, "Truly, I say to you, unless you turn and become
like children, you will never enter the kingdom of heaven."
(Matthew 18:2–3, RSV)

IN HER WITTY BOOK, *The Ten Commandments for
Grandparents,* Caryl Waller Krueger makes her sixth
commandment say, "You shall not continually give
gifts to your grandchildren." Although it is often
simpler to *buy* something for grandchildren instead of
be someone for them, it can become easy for your
grandchildren to think you are a gift. The "what did
you bring me" syndrome often makes grandchildren
more concerned with our *presents* than our *presence.*

Did you ever hear of grandchildren giving us gifts? I
am not speaking of material gifts at birthdays or Christmas, but the gift of childlike wonder and spontaneity.

My four year old grandson Daniel came with his
family to eat lunch at the retirement community where I
was delivering some lectures. He seemed overwhelmed
by all the gray-haired people and suddenly he blurted
out, "I never saw so many grandpas and grandmas in
all my life!" It was so spontaneous and exuberant that
all who heard laughed. It was a gift of a child to people
who needed that graceful touch of humor.

No wonder that when the disciples asked Jesus who
was the greatest in God's kingdom, he took a child and
said that unless they turned and became as a little child

they could not enter the kingdom. Jesus knew that the qualities of trust, wonder, innocence, and dependence are the pattern of the Christian's attitude towards God.

I received a precious gift from another grandson, Christopher. We went for a walk at twilight down a deserted suburban street. I was looking straight ahead, concerned about any possible danger and suddenly Christopher said, "Grandpa! Did you see that?" He pointed to the sky and said, "Look at the moon and stars. Aren't they lovely?"

I thought of Psalm 8, when the writer looked at the heavens and exclaimed, "When I look at your heavens, the work of your fingers, the moon and stars that you have established; what are human beings that you are mindful of them?" (8:3–4, NRSV). And the second verse came to mind, "Out of the mouths of babes and infants You have ordained strength." (8:2, NKJV). My grandson had given me a gift–to look up and see the beauty of God's world at night and to wonder at God's creation.

Children are a microcosm of the kingdom and if we spend time with them, they will shower us with gifts from their childlike eyes. Grandchildren are gifts from God. In a real sense we are reborn with each new grandchild. It is a gift of a new connection between all who have preceded us and all who proceed from them. No wonder the psalmist exclaimed, "The Lord bless you out of Zion; and may you see the good of Jerusalem, all the days of your life. Yes, may you see your children's children" (Psalm 128:5–6, NKJV).

GIVER OF ALL GOOD THINGS:
We praise you for the gift of children and grandchildren
that bless our lives with their Christlike spirits.
May we always cherish moments spent with them.
AMEN.

58

Is There Anything New in the Twenty-third Psalm?

READ PSALM 23

Is there a thing of which it is said, "See, this is new?"
It has been already, in the ages before us.
(Ecclesiastes 1:10, RSV)

Behold, I make all things new.
(Revelation 21:5, RSV)

WHO WOULD THINK one would find anything new in the Twenty-third Psalm? It has become so much a part of our spiritual lives that we let its beauty blind us to new truth. I thought I had exhausted its meaning years ago. I remembered reading: "Though I walk through the valley of the shadow of death, I will fear no evil." The *valley* of the shadow—not the shadow of death.

The valley of death is the moment of death itself as it is rightly so often named at funerals. But for all of life we walk through the valley over which the shadow of death moves. In the midst of life, we are in the midst of death, but we walk through it.

In one of my former parishes, a dear elderly woman told me that she had named two cats after the Twenty-third Psalm. "I named them Goodness and Mercy, and they follow me all the days of my life." At the end of his life, the old shepherd David could affirm that a gracious Providence had surrounded him all the days of his life.

My memory went back to a sermon I heard while I was a student in seminary and a story told by one of the students. A famous actor returned to his hometown to be honored for his achievements. Sitting in the audience was his old retired pastor. Someone asked the actor to recite the Twenty-third Psalm and he agreed if the old minister would do likewise. The actor recited the Psalm with great eloquence. The retired minister stumbled over the words, and left some of them out, but when he sat down, there was a silence in the banquet hall. The actor turned to his friend and said, "I know the Twenty-third Psalm but the minister knows the Shepherd!"

Is there anything new in the Twenty-third Psalm? Needless to say, it has spoken to people in all circumstances and situations. The living live by it and the dying die by it. It is both simply divine and divinely simple. There is always something new in the Twenty-third Psalm as it speaks to our situation. As one of the pilgrim fathers said, "There is always more light and truth to break forth from God's holy word."

My view is that David wrote this psalm in his latter years as a kind of life review. As he reflected on his life, he realized the gracious care and love that the Shepherd had for him. I heard of a Sunday school teacher who asked her group of children if anyone could quote the entire psalm. A golden-haired four-and-a-half year old girl was among those who raised their hands. A bit skeptical, the teacher asked her to try. The girl faced the class. "The Lord is my shepherd, that's all I want," she said. Something new from the Twenty-third Psalm.

We can make the same statement, "The Lord is my Shepherd; that's all I want."

GOOD SHEPHERD:
We praise you for your loving care all the days of our lives.
Surely your goodness has never failed us and
we shall always be secure in your mercy.
AMEN.

59

Looking Forward by Looking Back
READ DEUTERONOMY 8:1-20

Stand at the crossroads and look;
ask for the ancient paths, ask where the good way is, and
walk in it, and you will find rest for your souls.
(Jeremiah 6:16, NIV)

THROUGHOUT THE LATER HISTORY OF ISRAEL, the prophets constantly called upon the people to remember God's call and acts in their past. Isaiah told them, "Look to the rock from which you were cut and to the quarry from which you were hewn; look to Abraham, your father, and to Sarah, who gave you birth."(Isaiah 51:1–2, NIV). In remembering the God's call in their history, the people of Israel could understand that continuing call in their present. There was continuity between the call of God to them in their past and the call of God in the living moment of their history.

For some, retirement is disengagement, a time of withdrawal from life. For others, it is new activity. For those who seek to understand how God fits into retirement, we must return to see how God was at work in our past stories. Only then can we understand how God calls us in this new chapter of life's journey. There is continuity between how God called us in our past and how God calls us now.

Reflecting on how God called me, I recall how I was called to ministry, to be a caregiver, a wounded healer. Only as I recollected that call did I come to realize that God's continuing call in retirement has not drastically changed. God does not expect me to find some new, dramatic second career in the twilight years of life. Rather, God's call is to continued ministry with a special concern for the aging. Frederick Buechner wrote,

> It is the Lord, it is God, who has been with us through all our days and years whether we knew it or not, he sings—with us in our best moments and in our worst moments, to heal us with his wonders, to wound us healingly with his judgments, to bless us in hidden ways though more often than not we had forgotten his name.

Sometimes we are afraid to face our mortality, so we back into our future. Then we become immobilized by our past failures and sorrows. The result is a diminished present that is our own creation.

As we look backward and see God's presence in life, we can look forward to the end of life with hope and optimism. With Jacob, who perhaps never realized God's presence in his earlier days, we can affirm, "Surely the Lord is in this place, and I was not aware of it" (Genesis 28:16, NIV). That is the wisdom of standing at the crossroads of our lives, at retirement, and looking for the ancient paths.

GOD OF ALL AGES, PAST AND FUTURE:
*We begin to see connections now
between our past and your presence. Help us to believe that
coincidences are your work.*
AMEN.

60

The Right to Work
READ MARK 3:1-6

May the favor of the Lord our God rest upon us;
establish the work of our hands for us—
yes, establish the work of our hands.
(Psalm 90:17, NIV)

BY ALL REPORTS, the man with the withered arm was a stone mason. In restoring his hand, Jesus gave him back his work. The Gospel to the Hebrews reports the man's prayer: "I was a stone mason, seeking to earn my living with my hands; I pray you, Jesus, give me back my health that I may not have to beg my bread in shame."

Many people want to work past retirement. Some who chose early retirement want to get back to work. Others prefer partial employment. A sixty-two-year-old man, beaten down by endless efforts to find work, told me, "I've been rejected so many times I'm beginning to believe I am worthless. My friends tell me to 'Keep the faith,' and 'God will open a door,' but all of them have steady incomes or big pensions. How can they relate to me when I am so broke and in debt that I feel helpless?"

For some, the problem is age-old discrimination against older workers. For others, it is the unjust Social Security earnings test that limits the wages retirees can make and still collect benefits. The reality that there are some seniors who need to work needs to counter the belief that *all* seniors have little financial need to work. Despite their exodus from the work force, there are millions of retirees who would rather be working.

Workers with experience are especially needed in long-term health care areas. With the earnings limit in place, older people are discouraged from working, so health care facilities lose valuable, experienced workers.

Some argue that older persons should be discouraged from working so as to create jobs for younger people. But the pool of younger workers is shrinking and there will be labor shortages at the end of this century. We cannot afford to lose educated, skilled, experienced workers. Keeping seniors employed could also protect future generations from a crushing tax burden to finance Social Security and Medicare.

I discovered that partial employment past retirement is an excellent compromise, a healthy way to find that creative balance between action and rest. Parker Palmer asks a crucial question, "Why do some people who have retired from positions of power and visibility, people who have nothing left to prove, still sense the void when their 'active days' are over still need to justify themselves by rehearsing their achievements?"

Jesus had compassion on the man with the withered arm because of his disability *and* because it isolated him from the world of work. Modern society is being cast into the image of the ancient legalists who put the rigidity of the law above human need. Older workers who want to work should be employed for their own value not because it is good social policy. Older workers who have been getting the job done for years may prove to be pure gold in a few years.

COMPANION OF ALL WHO WORK:
We thank you for your grace and strength that
establishes the work of our hands. Be with all older workers,
that they may be delivered from discrimination, and not stand
idle in the marketplace at the eleventh hour.
AMEN.

VII

GOD'S CALL AT RETIREMENT

So our call;
consists of daily marching orders
rather than an initiation into a guild
from which we may never be released. . . .

There is not retirement from our calling,
even though we may retire from a
specific occupation.
We are called to love God and
to enjoy him forever.

PAUL B. MAVES

61

Retirement Is God's Call
READ EXODUS 3:1–10

I took you from the ends of the earth,
from its farthest corners I called you. I said, "You are my
servant"; I have chosen you and have not rejected you.
(Isaiah 41:9, NIV)

AT FIRST MOSES HAD NO IDEA that God would call him as the deliverer of his people. For forty years he had lived the quiet life of a shepherd in Midian, tending sheep and settling down to ordinary days. No doubt the long hours in the wilderness gave him time to brood over the plight of his people, and bitter memories of their bondage burned in his mind.

Suddenly, in the burning of a bush, his life changed, and this semi-retired life of a nomad would end. Yahweh was calling him to redirected life. The words shattered his placid existence. "So now, go. I am sending you to Pharaoh to bring my people the Israelites out of Egypt" (Exodus 3:10, NIV). What an awesome call–to forge a nation out of a group of slaves.

In the months before retirement an old hymn, "Christ of the Upward Way," kept resounding in my mind.

> Give me the heart to hear Your voice and
> will, That without fault or fear I may fulfill
> Your purpose with a glad and holy zest,
> Like one who would not bring less than the best.

Even then God was calling me to this new journey of faith, though I did not realize it. At first my thoughts centered on my needs, and I imagined I would settle down into a quiet life style, in some green pasture of my own choosing. In retrospect, I realize that retirement is God's call to renewed service in the Third Age.

It is strange to think of God's call at retirement. We think of a calling at the dawn of a person's career or even at mid-life, when people shift gears and take other directions. But I am convinced that God also calls at retirement, into larger and greater opportunities. As Simone de Beauvoir wrote, "There is only one solution if old age is not to be an absurd parody of our former life, and that is to go on pursuing ends that give our existence a meaning—devotion to individuals, to groups or to causes, social, political, and to intellectual or creative work."

I am not sure yet what God's will is for these retirement years, but I am sure God has called me to some continuing ministry in aging. At present, I find that call in listening to faith stories of older persons and in training people to minister to the frail elderly through listening, compassion, and active caring.

> Christ calls us now, as long ago
> Beside the Galilee,
> The call went out to common folk,
> "Come now; come follow me."
> So, when we hear, respond, and go,
> We too must leave behind
> The trappings and encumbrances
> Possessing life and mind.
> –From "Christ Calls Us Now, as Long Ago"

GOD WHO CALLS:
Thank you for the call to further service and ministry at the eleventh hour of life. Give us grace to respond and obey, using these days for your glory.
AMEN.

62

Between the Devil and the Deep Blue Sea
READ EXODUS 14:5-18

They mounted up to heaven, they went down to the depths;
their courage melted away in their evil plight;
they. . . were at their wits' end.
(Psalm 107:26–27, RSV)

THOSE ANCIENT PEOPLE were still walking on clouds as they marched on toward the sea of reeds on their way to a promised land. Suddenly there was panic. Their illusions about an easy escape where shattered by the sight of 600 of Pharaoh's best chariots rushing to destroy them.

They thought it was the end. In front of them was the sea. Behind them, the power of the Pharaoh. Hemmed in, they focused their anger on Moses. "Was it because there were no graves in Egypt that you brought us out to the desert to die? . . . It would have been better for us to serve the Egyptians than die in the desert!" (Exodus 14:11–12, NIV). Between the devil and the deep blue sea.

In the last days before retirement, I felt as trapped as those ancient Israelites. I knew I had to retire, since I wanted to avoid the burnout that awaited me. The time had come to be free of the distress that was affecting my well being. As that ancient people felt the threat of Pharaoh's power, so I knew the inevitable cost of remaining in full time work. Furthermore, there would be no more career opportunities for one who bore two stigmas–reaching older age and being a healed victim of divorce. I could not go back. I felt terror about going through with retirement. The unknown sea terrified me. I developed all kinds of fears about life threatening diseases. I underwent tests to assure me that I did not suffer from some terminal illness. Like the ancient psalmist, I felt I was at my wits' end.

I needed to hear what Moses told those fearful slaves, "Do not be afraid. Stand firm and you will see the deliverance the LORD will bring you today. . . . The LORD will fight for you; you need only to be still" (Exodus 14:13–14, NIV). But I looked at the turbulent waves, not at the One who brings peace to our storm-tossed lives.

I did hear that strangest of all words, "Tell the Israelites to move on" (v.15). Where? Into the sea? There was nowhere else to go. I learned that "if you can't get out of it, get into it," and so I plunged into this new experience. I had to find a way even when there seemed to be no way. I had to move on even when all my possibilities for the future appeared blocked.

When life traps you between the devil and the deep blue sea, what saves you is that Voice from beyond, whose presence brings a deep peace. So, I moved with continuing apprehension into the sea.

———————

GOD OF ALL TIMES AND PLACES:
If ever we needed your help,
it is when we are trapped between the devil and the deep blue
sea. When life closes in on us, help us to look to you
and find the way through.
AMEN.

63

No Shortcuts to Redirection
READ EXODUS 13:17-22

When Pharaoh had let the people go,
God did not let them take the road to the land of the
Philistines, although that was the nearest way. . . . Instead,
God led the people by the roundabout way
of the wilderness to the Sea of Reeds.
(Exodus 13:17–18, JB)

IT SEEMED INCREDIBLE THAT MOSES led the Israelites out of Egypt by the roundabout way of the wilderness instead of the more direct road. If they had taken the shortcut up the coastal highway, they might have made it to the promised land in ten walking days. But God knew that along that coast there were Philistine cities and that those undisciplined, untrained Hebrew slaves would have been no match for their enemies.

"No shortcuts" is something that cuts across the grain of our American lifestyle. This is the age of instant coffee, instant cereal, instant success–instant everything. We have moved mountains with a single blast, hurled satellites into space, and prevented sickness with a single shot. But there is no instant success in the spiritual life. The discipline of the desert is necessary if we are to enter our destiny.

There are no shortcuts to fulfillment in the retirement journey either. I was naive enough to think retirement would be a piece of cake. I had relieved my financial worries and didn't have to relocate. Surely happiness would arrive with the first social security check. How wrong I was. It has been a wilderness journey, a time of danger and opportunity. I had to work through my emotions to grow through suffering and change.

I heard the story that the great opera singer Roberta Peters began to prepare for her career at the age of thirteen and devoted herself single-mindedly to that goal. At sixteen she was offered a role in a Broadway musical. The salary was attractive, but she would have to be away from her training for a year. She asked advice from a high school teacher who told her, "If you take this detour, you'll never know how far along the straight road you might have gone." She refused the shortcut, and four years later made her opera debut in Mozart's *Don Giovanni*.

The Hebrew people had much to struggle through in the wilderness: quarreling among themselves, rebellion against the leaders, family disputes, constant grumbling about the "vast and terrible wilderness" (Deuteronomy 1:10). Somehow, the experience built character. And somehow retirement can be a time of growth, when we learn to grow through discipline and suffering.

Jesus knew the value of the wilderness. His responses to the temptation to take the shortcut to his mission were all quoted from the wilderness scriptures of Deuteronomy. (See Matthew 4:1-11.) We remember that "although he was a Son, he learned obedience through what he suffered" (Hebrews 5:8, RSV).

In our wilderness, we are strengthened by the caring presence of God who journeys with us. But there are no shortcuts, there is only sacrifice.

REDEEMER OF ISRAEL:
*In your wisdom you led your people through the wilderness
and refused to allow them to take the easy way.
Help us to walk the narrow way which leads to life.*
AMEN.

64

Retirement Exodus
READ JOHN 8:31-36

*Jesus then said to the Jews who had believed in him,
"If you continue in my word, you are truly my disciples, and
you will know the truth, and the truth will make you free."
(John 8:31–32, RSV)*

THE HEBREWS' EXODUS FROM EGYPT meant deliverance from the tyranny of Pharaoh. The song of Miriam expressed this new-found freedom. "Sing to the LORD, for he has triumphed gloriously; the horse and his rider he has thrown into the sea" (Exodus 15:21, RSV).

The Jews could not understand Jesus' words about freedom, since they thought "they had never been in bondage to anyone" (obviously forgetting their history). But Jesus was speaking about slavery to sin and a freedom that gives an inner exodus. The ancient exodus from Egypt is the story of every person who faces bondage, who moves from a place of non-freedom to a place of real freedom.

In retrospect I realize how much I was in bondage to my work. It was an addiction in a culture too eager to reward such addiction. I was a genuine workaholic. Such people exhibit the same characteristics of addiction found in a drug addict or a compulsive gambler. "Essentially workaholics are no longer 'showing up' for life. . . . They have been taken over by the compulsion to work and are slaves to it. They no longer own their lives. They are truly the walking dead," writes Diane Fassel.

No one is exempt from the addiction to work. Even Thomas Merton, the twentieth century writer and monk, once wrote: "I have fallen into the great indignity, I have written against–I am a contemplative who is ready to collapse from overwork. This, I think, is a sin and the punishment of sin but now I have got to turn it to good use and be a saint by it somehow."

Workaholism is a sin, and Jesus' words ring true, "Everyone who commits sin is a slave to sin" (John 8:34, RSV). I tried to avoid dealing with my addiction by denial. After all, I had every reason to work so hard. Later I knew I was in bondage and out of balance. I experienced the truth of Paul's words, "I do not understand what I do. For what I want to do I do not do, but what I hate I do. . . . Who will rescue me from this body of death?" (Romans 7:15, 24, NIV).

For me, deliverance came in rediscovering the doctrine of salvation by grace. Retirement has meant that I am now out of Egypt–I am free, no longer driven by work or addicted to action. It is difficult to find life more abundant when one is working one's self to death.

I still find joy in healthy work. But now work is only one component of my redirected life, not its master. The ancient Israelite reenacted the exodus experience as he imagined he himself had come forth from Egypt. I can identify with the Exodus now since my redirected life has liberated me from my old taskmaster.

LIBERATING GOD:
Let what you began in us
come to fulfillment at the day of Jesus Christ.
Let us exult in the good news that we are accepted and
approved by your love, not by our work.
AMEN.

65

Living by Grace
READ EXODUS 16:1-21

*But he said to me, "My grace is sufficient for you,
for my power is made perfect in weakness."
(2 Corinthians 12:9, RSV)*

ISRAEL GOES INTO THE DESERT TO LIVE ON MANNA. It is little wonder that they clamored for Egypt. Anything rather than dependence on something upon which they had no claim. This manna was strange food, at best, even though it was a gift from Yahweh. They did not even know exactly what it was. But it taught them to live by grace.

The apostle Paul prayed ceaselessly that his "thorn in the flesh" would be taken from him. The physical affliction caused him endless days and nights of pain and impeded his work. The answer to Paul's prayer was, "My grace is sufficient for you." God did not take the thorn away but rather gave Paul strength to bear it.

In retirement years, we learn to live by grace. No longer are we defined by what we do or find affirmation in our work. The event of retirement empties out of a person's life his or her sturdy crutch of self-worth—our social role or usefulness. In this moment of being stripped of our former lifestyle, we can discover the gospel. No one earns their way: All that we are or have is a gift of God, all is grace. So the author of the fourth Gospel can exclaim, "from his fulness we all received grace upon grace" (John 1:16, RSV).

No person in Christian history more exemplifies the work of grace than John Newton, the great evangelical preacher of the eighteenth century. His early years were one continuous round of rebellion. He became a captain of his own slave ship, collecting slaves for sale to visiting traders. On March 10, 1748, while returning to England from Africa during a stormy voyage, when it appeared that all would be lost, Newton began reading *The Imitation of Christ* by Thomas à Kempis. His conversion led to a changed life. He became a strong and effective crusader against slavery and for fifteen years served as a parish minister in the little village of Olney, near Cambridge, England. His 1779 hymn, "Amazing Grace," summarizes his life under grace,

> Amazing grace! How sweet the sound
> That saved a wretch like me!
> I once was lost, but now am found;
> Was blind, but now I see.
>
> Through may dangers, toils, and snares,
> I have already come;
> 'Tis grace hath brought me safe thus far,
> And grace will lead me home.

This might well be the official retirement hymn, for it reminds us that life is a gift, that we are accepted by the grace of God, and that God's grace is sufficient.

GOD OF GRACE:
It is you who have chosen, preserved, guided, and strengthened us—all through your grace. In these years of retirement, may we live by that grace.
AMEN.

66

Back to Egyptland
READ NUMBERS 14:3-10

Would it not be better for us to go back to Egypt?
(Numbers 14:3, RSV)

A RECURRING THEME in the story of Israel's journey is "back to Egypt." Virtually moments after experiencing Yahweh's power over the Pharaoh, with memories of the Passover and the escape from Egypt still fresh in their hearts, they wanted to go back to Egypt. They cried to Moses, "What have you done to us by bringing us out of Egypt? . . . It would have been better for us to serve the Egyptians than die in the desert" (Exodus 14:11–12, NIV).

Later in the journey, with memories of deliverance at the sea and provision for their needs in the wilderness, they panicked at a report of giants in the land. "Wouldn't it be better for us to go back to Egypt?" (Numbers 14:3, NIV). Their wail was a cry for the security of Egyptland. They preferred being slaves to facing the terrifying freedom of the wilderness.

Back to Egyptland–I know the feeling. I find myself over-involved with volunteer work in the community. "Let Dick do it," is the constant refrain. I joined the thousands of other retirees who suddenly become prime targets for all kinds of community service, simply because we are retired. Volunteer work is rewarding and offers a rich supply of service to the community. But it can also cause problems.

My over-involvement in volunteer work created within me a desire to go back to work. I began to realize how much I missed the activity, the reassuring words and kindnesses of people I helped, and the support of colleagues. Even the difficult conflicts had helped me grow in grace. I found it hard to admit I was retired, no longer in the mainstream. I gave serious thought to going back and returning to my former life.

"No one who puts his hand to the plow and looks back is fit for the kingdom of God" (Luke 9:62, RSV). There was no turning back. I could not make a mockery of all this struggle to be where I am. The loneliness of freedom was better than the former comfortable prison. I knew then that there was no return. My hand was on the plow.

The last verse of Annie Johnson Flint's poem became a daily source of strength.

> But God hath promised
> Strength for the day,
> Rest for the labor,
> Light for the way.
> Grace for the trials.
> Help from above,
> Unfailing sympathy,
> Undying love.

GOD OF ALL TIMES AND PLACES:
You are with us in those moments of weakness when we want to go back instead of forward. You are greater than our hearts and do not condemn us for our shortcomings.
Give us courage to face our unknowns.
AMEN.

67

Mired at Marah

READ EXODUS 15:22-27

When they came to Marah,
they cold not drink the water of Marah because it was bitter.
(Exodus 15:23, NRSV)

FOR THREE DAYS THE ISRAELITES WANDERED in the wilderness of Shur beneath the relentless sun. Their joy at the deliverance from Pharaoh now seemed a pyrrhic victory. Facing the barren, dry wasteland, they wondered where they could find water. They found it at Marah, but could not drink it because it was bitter. God heard the prayer of Moses and the water is sweetened. Finally they reach an oasis at Elim, where they discover the twelve springs of Elim and water enough for all.

In *The Exodus Experience*, Maureena Fritz says "In the spiritual journey, Marah and Shur stand for periods of trial. Marah means 'bitterness,' the bitterness that comes from frustrated goodwill and the feeling of being betrayed by God. The wilderness of Shur represents the emptiness that is experienced when the trappings of the outside world are left behind."

I discovered that my newfound freedom had its wilderness of Shur and waters of Marah. It was liberating to be freed from the distress of work and given new freedom in my Third Age. But it wasn't long before the wilderness took hold. Empty days became the routine.

We can get mired at Marah and become grumblers and complainers in the wilderness. But at Marah, God gave the Israelites a rule of disciplined, diligent listening to God's word and faithful following of that word.

The early days of retirement brought some bitter experiences for me. Feeling out of the mainstream of life, with everything passing me by, made me feel as though I had been put on the shelf. Some of the feelings may have been my own problem, but the fact remains that in a society that still gives priority to production and achievement, retirement brings loneliness.

Yet it was at Marah that God led me to the enduring rule of faithful meditation on God's word and the wisdom of the psalmist's words, "But his delight is in the law of the Lord, and on his law he meditates day and night" (1:2). Entering into this wilderness was being drawn more deeply into the mystery of God's presence and love. In time, I too discovered the springs of Elim, where the living water flowed freely. Is not Marah a shining symbol of all of life? The bitter experiences that cause us pain can become the very moments when God leads us through the wilderness.

One of my cherished friends is Aunt Mayme Carpenter of Summerville, South Carolina. She is in her Fourth Age and still writing poetry at the age of ninety-nine. When she went through the bitterness of losing her husband, she wrote the poem below. It might well become anyone's prayer when they come to Marah.

GIVE ME STRENGTH, O LORD, I PRAY
To do Thy will for this one day.
Give me strength to bear my sorrow,
Strengthen my faith in a new tomorrow.
You alone know the depth of my grief
And only You can give relief.
So please dear God, have compassion on me,
And hold me a little bit closer to Thee.
AMEN.

68

Encouraged in the Struggle
READ EXODUS 17:8-16

But Moses' arms grew heavy, so they took a stone and put it under him and on this he sat, Aaron and Hur supporting his arms, one on one side, one on the other; and his arms remained firm until sunset.
(Exodus 17:12, JB)

WHAT A SCENE. God's people are in battle with the Amalekites. Moses is standing on a hill above the conflict, his arms outstretched in prayer for a victory. When his arms grew heavy, Aaron and Hur held up his hands. The silhouette of Moses' intercession serves as a mark of faith to the warriors below, and they win the battle. The battle was crucial for survival and to fire their determination to continue on their journey of faith. It was all hinged on Moses' prayer; as long as his arms were raised to heaven, they would prevail, but it took the help of his kinsmen to remain steadfast until sunset.

Early in my retirement, I discovered my arms grew weary as I battled enemies within me and those in the way. My impatience, self-doubt, and anxiety about the future could have forced me to return to full-time work or become overwhelmed by despair. I soon realized how important was the encouragement of family and friends, especially during these autumn years.

William Clements tells about a respected teacher who retired and was given an office at the university. You might expect that students would flock to seek his wisdom, but he was politely ignored. How sad. As a retired man once said to me, "In the latter years of my life, I finally have some answers. But nobody asks me any questions."

The loss of defined roles and the sense that my life makes a difference happens to most who retire. It is not necessarily due to a sense of failure, it is an inevitable result of growing older. Perhaps we need to be thinking of shedding some of our roles, as a caterpillar sheds its husk to become a butterfly, rather than thinking that retirement is the end of our existence.

I came to deeply appreciate the encouragement of my family and colleagues. They held up my arms in my endless struggles against the demons in the wilderness. My wife has been my greatest encourager, standing with me and offering me her presence in the difficult days.

Other encouragers have come to my side. Old friends, colleagues in ministry who have not forgotten, Third Agers who call and encourage, and Fourth Agers with whom I share life stories–all have been a constant source of hope.

Rollo Mays wrote, "Understanding . . . draws the other human being for a moment out of [their] individual existence and welcomes [them] into community. It is like inviting the traveler in from [their] snowy and chilly journey to warm [themselves] for an hour for an hour before the fire on another's hearth." And that is a great image for older people, who too often feel trapped in the wintry, chilly journey of retirement.

REDEEMER OF THE WEARY:
We can become too easily discouraged in our daily battles of the soul. We thank you for the availability of friends, but most of all we thank you for your constant presence.
AMEN.

69

The Retirement Dance
READ EXODUS 32:1-6
& 2 SAMUEL 6:1-15

*And they rose early on the morrow,
and offered burnt offerings and brought peace offerings; and
the people sat down to eat and drink and rose up to play.
(Exodus 32:6, RSV)*

I READ YESTERDAY ABOUT THE DANCE EXCHANGE, an international dance troupe that teaches dance-type movement to blind older people, many in wheelchairs. A seventy-year-old member says, "It is a fascinating thing. It causes you to get in touch with your best spirit." For these Third Agers, their dance step is not the one-two, one-two kind of dance so many are used to. New movements focus on imagination and a sense of fun.

Dancing can be a good form of exercise and enjoyment for retired persons. Surely we have a good role model in David who "danced before the Lord with all his might" when the ark was brought to Jerusalem! However, in another moment in Israel's history, some raucous dancing was not so productive. Moses had climbed Mount Sinai to be with Yahweh. At the foot of this same mountain, the people of Israel had taken two steps forward. They had come from slavery in Egypt and had entered into a covenant with Yahweh, to be his peculiar people. And then, despairing at Moses' absence, tired of a god they could not see, they built a golden calf and danced before the idol. When

Moses approached the camp and saw the calf and the dancing, he broke the commandments at the foot of the mountain. Two steps forward, one step backwards. The retirement dance.

I have felt good about my decision to retire, to be freed from the stress, and have actually enjoyed leisure for the first time since the halcyon days of childhood. One of my retired friends shared a slogan with me: *Life is two periods of play interrupted by forty years of work.*

I feel no guilt about the leisure. It is not unproductive or misspent time. Jesus never confined his life to ceaseless work. Even in those pressured public years, he withdrew and took time for spiritual and renewal. He counseled us to "See how the lilies of the field grow. They do not labor or spin" (Matthew 6:28, NIV).

However, leisure is not the highest good in these retirement years. God's call doesn't end at retirement nor does ministry terminate with the retirement ceremony–God's call is for life. And as long as I maintain my health and energy level, I am not content with a life of leisure. The retirement dance is 2-1, 2-1. Two steps forward, and one backward.

The words of Charles Wesley's "A Charge to Keep I Have" keeps pounding at my heart:

> To serve the present age,
> My calling to fulfill;
> O may it all my powers engage,
> To do my Master's will!

GOD OF THE MORNING. NOON, AND EVENING OF LIFE,
We cannot believe that your call is only
for the morning and noon of our lives. In the evening of life,
we hear you calling still. Help us to listen and obey.
AMEN.

70

Off the Briar and on the Wing
READ DEUTERONOMY 32:10-14

---

*Like an eagle that stirs up its nest and hovers over its young,
that spreads its wings to catch them and carries them on its
pinions. . . . the LORD alone led him.*
(Deuteronomy 32:11–12, NIV)

THE HEBREWS HAD SETTLED IN at the foot of Mount
Sinai. There they had received the words of the law, the
pattern of the tabernacle, and the ritual for worship.
But, swiftly and suddenly the word of Yahweh came to
them, "You have stayed long enough at this mountain"
(Deuteronomy 1:6, NIV). It was time to get off the briar
and get on the wing.

Later, Moses compared God's marching orders to the
way in which the mother eagle encourages her young to
fly–as an eagle stirs up its nest. The mother eagle flings
the eaglets out of the nest. They are comfortable there
but they will never fly if they remain there. They begin
to fall, struggling in the air, but the mother eagle
catches them on her wings. Finally, they learn to fly.

All through life, God initiates change. As we grow
older, we become more settled and resist change. Like
the young eaglets, safe and comfortable in their soft
nest high among the rocks, we want to be left alone. We
want things to stay the way they are. We want to settle
down into some situation that we are used to and not be
disturbed or uprooted. But God disturbs our settled life.
God deliberately destroys our complacency and teases
us with the irritant of change. When the mother eagle

breaks up the nest, she is trying to give her eaglets real security–not the security of a rotting nest but the security of wings; not the security that depends on outward circumstances but one that comes from inner power. God creates change so that we may cultivate the power to align ourselves with the things that are above and claim our heritage in the skies.

Only later did I realize that the discontent and struggle of the retirement process was all part of God's way of disturbing my life. It is only when the nest is stirred that we learn to fly.

These verses from Deuteronomy suggest another great truth. The mother eagle never deserts her brood after the nest is stirred. When they start to fall, she swoops beneath them, catching them on her own strong wings, bearing them back to the nest on the rocky ledge. Israel learned that it was Yahweh who bore them on eagles' wings and brought them to himself. (See Exodus 19:4.)

In the difficult days of learning new directions, we do stumble and fall. But God does not desert us and we learn that underneath are the everlasting arms. When our resources are exhausted, God supports us and gives us strength. So even in these more settled days, when life seems secure in the nest, God is disturbing us that we may fly to new heights.

―――――――

ETERNAL FATHER-MOTHER GOD:
*Our tendency is to want to settle down
and claim our comfort in these retirement years.
Disturb us and shake us out of our nests, that we may find
new ways to serve you.*
AMEN.

71

The View from Mount Nebo

READ DEUTERONOMY 34:1-12

*These all died in faith,
not having received what was promised, but having seen it
and greeted it from afar, and having acknowledged that
they were strangers and exiles on the earth.*
(Hebrews 11:13, RSV)

MOSES SPENT THE LAST FORTY YEARS OF HIS LIFE trying to
forge a nation out of an army of ex-slaves. He saw the
land of promise but never entered it. Moses died on a
lonely mountain without actually reaching the goal he'd
been striving toward for nearly half a century. The
poorest child of the people who entered the land had
what Moses would never have.

One tradition suggests that Moses was prevented
from entering the promised land because he struck a
rock to obtain water from it, after God instructed him
merely to speak to it. (See Numbers 20:10-13.) Another
says that he wasn't allowed to cross the river because of
the sins of the Israelites. (See Deuteronomy. 3:26–27.)

There is something symbolic in this view from Mount
Nebo. None of us ever accomplishes everything we
want to accomplish, no matter how long and how hard
we work at it. As long as we live, there will always be
another mountain to climb, another river to cross,
another place to go. That seems to fly in the face of what
we have been taught by our culture. We've been taught
to finish what we start, to tie up loose ends, to get
closure on projects and relationships. But this story of

Moses on Mount Nebo reminds us that there will always be unfinished business in life. "Ah, but a man's reach should exceed his grasp, or what's a heaven for?" Robert Browning writes in "Andrea Del Sarto."

The writer to the Hebrews knew it too, for his words were written for us, as well as for the ancient Israelites. We too die in faith as strangers and exiles on the earth. Joseph Sittler says that there is another perspective to be seen from Mount Nebo from which one can envision the Christian faith. "The people of Mount Nebo are the obedient children of both participation and detachment. They know and they do not know fully. . . . On the peak of Nebo, between participation without substance and detachment without peace, they add their astringent voice to the song of faith."

The view from Mount Nebo is actually a word of comfort for our later years. We never reach the goal, the joy is found in the journey. We see the promised land but never enter it. So we trust God with the unfinished business that we have to leave behind. The words of Jane Parker Huber's hymn, "God, You Spin the Whirling Planets," reflect the same thought:

> God, Your word is still creating,
> Calling us to life made new.
> Now reveal to us fresh vistas
> Where there's work to dare and do.
> Keep us clear of all distortion
> Polish us with loving care.
> Thus, new creatures in Your image,
> We'll proclaim Christ everywhere.

―――――――――

REDEEMING GOD:
You alone will bring to completion what we have begun;
help us to trust you with life's unfinished business.
AMEN.

72

Making Sense of Our Memories
READ EXODUS 13:1-16

*In days to come, when your son asks you, "What does this
mean?" say to him, "With a mighty hand the LORD brought
us out of Egypt, out of the land of slavery."
(Exodus 13:14, NIV)*

THE PASSOVER FEAST BEGINS WITH A CHILD ASKING
"What does this mean?" and then the precious memory
of Israel's deliverance from Egypt is retold and reenacted. For the Hebrew, to remember is more than to
just recall the past; it is to make that past powerfully
present, in such a way that it influences the present life.
Hebrews never refer to the people of the ancient story
as *they*, it is always *we*.

In the Eucharist, we reenact this sacred meal in Jesus'
memory. But it is more than a memorial of a past event.
It puts us in touch with a living presence. The
remembering is so powerful that we experience that
meal as if we were present.

One of the tasks during retirement years is that of
preserving our stories. Telling our stories is a good way
to hand on our faith to the next generation. As the
psalmist said, "things we have heard and known,
things our fathers told us. We will not hide them from
our children; we will tell the next generation the
praiseworthy deeds of the LORD, his power, and the
wonders he has done" (78:3–4, NIV).

The telling of our faith stories is a spiritual act. We
not only collect our memories but recall our lives before

God. It is a way of finding the pattern or design of our lives, especially if we can see the hand of God in them. It is like standing on the bow of a ship in the middle of an ocean. Looking ahead we cannot tell the direction of the ship. But if we move to the stern and see the pattern of the wake, we can discover the course of the ship by seeing where we have been. Recollecting our stories helps us to understand God's care and providence at work in them.

Everyone wants to feel that his or her life has counted for something, that from the scattered fragments of their lives some meaning has emerged. But we are an unfinished story. As Paula Farrell Sullivan writes, "The portrait of our lives remains unfinished until we breathe for the last time. . . . With us into that gentle night will go the Holy Mystery that carries us through every word of our story."

That "Holy Mystery" is the redeeming note of my story. It has carried me–redeeming my failures, enabling my successes, and providing a presence that has sustained me throughout life. Now I know what the author of the Psalm 73 meant:

> Yet I am always with you;
>   you hold me by my right hand.
> You guide me with your counsel,
>   and afterward you will take me into glory.
> Whom have I in heaven but you?
>   And being with you, I desire nothing on earth.

LOVING GOD:
*As we think back over our days,
we are filled with wonder at your loving and faithful care.
Indeed, you have been our strength and stay.*
AMEN.

73

I Can See Clearly Now
READ MARK 8:22-26

The man, who was beginning to see, replied,
"I can see people; they look like trees to me, but they are
walking about." Then [Jesus] laid his hands on the man's eyes
again and he saw clearly; he was cured, and he could see
everything plainly and distinctly.
(Mark 8:24–25, JB)

IN THE STORY OF THE HEALING OF THE BLIND MAN at Bethsada, Jesus' attempt to heal him is not immediately successful. At first, he could see people, but they looked more like trees walking. It took a second touch by the Master before he saw clearly.

I confess that the early days of my retirement resembled this story of the blind man. I could see only dimly what retirement would be like. *Webster's* defines retirement as "retiring or state of being retired; retreat as of an army; withdrawal into seclusion. . . ." It took a second touch to be able to see it clearly.

I realize now that it is a journey, not a destination. I pray Thomas Merton's prayer from *Thoughts in Solitude*. "My Lord God, I have no idea where I am going. I do not see the road ahead of me. I cannot know for certain where it will end. Nor do I really know myself, and the fact that I think I am following your will does not mean that I am actually doing so. But I believe that the desire to please you does in fact please you. And I hope that I have that desire in all that I am doing."

My journey goes on but I can see clearly now. At first it was like a series of reflections in a broken window. It made no sense. I have come a long way from my old workaholic life. I have learned to pace myself, enjoy nature and music, and take time for solitude. And, finally, I can let God take charge of my journey.

I am discovering the fragile balance between time for vital involvement and time for prayer. I still find joy in creating, not for the approval of others or some material reward, but for the sheer love of bringing something out of nothing. I am more honest with people and less afraid of what other people think about me. I am free from conforming to others' expectations or demands.

In the biblical story, it is significant that Christ did not heal the blind man immediately but walked with him in his blindness, guiding him before the healing was complete. And it took multiple touches before he saw clearly. In retrospect I realize that is my story too, as God in Christ walked with me in my blindness, before I could see clearly that retirement can become a time of vital involvement and creative prayer.

I recall some words from Robert Pirsig's book, *Zen and the Art of Motorcycle Maintenance*:

> Trials never end of course. Unhappiness and misfortune are bound to occur as long as people live, but there is a feeling now, that was not here before, and is not just on the surface of things, but penetrates all the way through. We've won it. It's going to get better now. You can sort of tell these things.

———————

LIGHT OF ALL SEEING:
Thank you for touching my eyes a second time
so I might realize that retirement can be a time of redirection
and of joy at the close of the day.
AMEN.

74

I Never Found That Rocking Chair

READ JOSHUA 14:6-14

So here I am today, eighty-five years old!
I am still as strong today as the day Moses sent me out . . .
Now give me this hill country that the LORD
promised me that day.
(Joshua 14:10–12, NIV)

EVEN AT HIS RIPE OLD AGE, Caleb was not ready for a rocking chair or a tent in some retirement village in the Jordan Valley. Some may have thought that it was the time for his disengagement from life, but he claimed a mountain. He asked for a challenge, not a cushion. He wanted more adventures in his "retirement" years.

More and more, I am beginning to realize what this journey of retirement means. At first I was anxious that I would be discarded and abandoned. Then I enjoyed the first freedom of doing nothing and later discovered that I still had to be involved. My need for people and projects made me plunge headlong into a "butterfly existence," flitting from one distraction to another.

There were times when I was tempted to return to my work but through struggle and prayer decided to let go of that past and find a new identity. And that has happened.

I have learned to find a delicate balance between vital involvement and quiet solitude. I cherish my privacy, my quiet time, and precious moments for meditation. I have learned how to stay vitally involved, and yet have none of the old passion for performance or anxious concerns about other people's expectations or demands. I have learned not to be trapped by the distress of bearing burdens *for* others, instead of *with* them. I rejoice in new challenges, and projects. I know now that spirituality means a way of living in depth; active caring and compassion balanced by passive quiet and meditation.

In his memorable words, Father Donald X. Burt expresses my penultimate thoughts for these retirement years:

> The brevity of my life dictates that I must not waste it. At the same time I must not take it too seriously. I must not grasp at it as though it were indeed the "end all and be all" of my existence. . . .
>
> . . . when I end here I am really just beginning. At death I will not even have *begun* to unravel the golden thread that is the rest of my life.

Retirement is not a destination, it is a journey, one that began almost two years ago for me. I am just now beginning to find what God intends for the rest of my life. I know that I will neither rust out nor rush about. Life is no flickering ember for me, but a splendid torch which I want to make burn as brightly as possible.

I never found that rocking chair. And I am so glad.

GOD OF MANY DELIVERANCES:
You have delivered me from my fears and anxieties
and led me to the Rock that is higher than I.
Give me courage to hold fast to what I have found in you.
Keep me pressing on toward that upward call
until life's end and beyond.
AMEN.